Go Crochet!
Afghan Design Workbook

50 motifs • **10** projects
1 of a kind results

Ellen Gormley

kp

KRAUSE PUBLICATIONS
CINCINNATI, OHIO

Go Crochet! Afghan Design Workbook Copyright © 2011 by Ellen Gormley. Manufactured in China. All rights reserved. No part of this book may be reproduced in any form or by any electronic or mechanical means including information storage and retrieval systems without permission in writing from the publisher, except by a reviewer who may quote brief passages in a review. Published by Krause Publications, a division of F+W Media, Inc., 4700 East Galbraith Road, Cincinnati, Ohio, 45236. (800) 289-0963. First Edition.

Other fine Krause Publications titles are available from your local bookstore, craft supply store, online retailer or visit our website at www.fwmedia.com.

www.fwmedia.com

15 14 13 12 11   5 4 3 2 1

DISTRIBUTED IN CANADA BY FRASER DIRECT
100 Armstrong Avenue
Georgetown, ON, Canada L7G 5S4
Tel: (905) 877-4411

DISTRIBUTED IN THE U.K. AND EUROPE BY F+W MEDIA INTERNATIONAL
Brunel House, Newton Abbot, Devon, TQ12 4PU, England
Tel: (+44) 1626 323200, Fax: (+44) 1626 323319
Email: postmaster@davidandcharles.co.uk

DISTRIBUTED IN AUSTRALIA BY CAPRICORN LINK
P.O. Box 704, S. Windsor NSW, 2756 Australia
Tel: (02) 4577-3555

Library of Congress Cataloging in Publication Data
Gormley, Ellen
  Go crochet! : afghan design workbook : 50 motifs, 10 projects, 1 of a kind results / Ellen Gormley.
     p. cm.
  Includes index.
  ISBN-13: 978-1-4402-0907-9 (hardcover : alk. paper)
  1. Afghans (Coverlets) 2. Crocheting--Patterns. I. Title.
  TT825.G596 2011
  746.43'0437--dc22
                        2010040635

Edited by **Kelly Biscopink**
Designed by **Kelly O'Dell**
Production coordinated by **Greg Nock**
Photography by **Christine Polomsky** and **Al Parrish**
Photo Styling by **Lauren Emmerling**
Illustrated by **Karen Manthey**

METRIC CONVERSION CHART

To convert	to	multiply by
Inches	Centimeters	2.54
Centimeters	Inches	0.4
Feet	Centimeters	30.5
Centimeters	Feet	0.03
Yards	Meters	0.9
Meters	Yards	1.1

ABOUT THE AUTHOR

Ellen began crocheting when she was ten years old. Her fondest crochet memory is stitching a blanket with her mother for her grandmother's birthday. Ellen can't remember who taught her to crochet, but she believes that it seeped into her consciousness from an early age from her great-aunt, Tanta Margaret, who resided next door.

Ellen abandoned crochet as a teenager only to pick it back up again while in graduate school at the University of Cincinnati. She has crocheted obsessively ever since, stitching more than eighty afghans before beginning her design career in 2004. Now, Ellen has sold more than one hundred designs. She has been published numerous times in many crochet magazines, including *Interweave Crochet*, *Crochet Today*, *Crochet!*, *Crochet World* and *Inside Crochet*. Her designs have been shown on PBS's *NeedleArts Studio with Shay Pendray* and *Knit and Crochet Now!* In 2008, Ellen was voted the Best Crochet Designer of Home Décor by the Crochet Liberation Front.

When not crocheting, Ellen enjoys reading, knitting, Jazzercise and chocolate cake. Ellen lives near Cincinnati with her husband, Tom, and their two children.

You can follow Ellen on her blog at www.GoCrochet.com and as GoCrochet on Twitter, Crochetville and Ravelry.

DEDICATION

To my husband, Tom, who tolerates my yarn and talks about me with pride behind my back…

To my gorgeous, smart daughter, Maura, who wears my crocheted gifts with pride. You're my best model.

To my handsome, brave son, Patrick, my superhero, "Nudge Monster", who nudges the cat away from the yarn.

I love you bunches, I love you to infinity, I love you more than chocolate cake.

ACKNOWLEDGMENTS

• Thank you to my family who finds me by following snippets of yarn scattered throughout the house like bread crumbs in the forest.

• Thank you to acquisitions and foster editor, Jenni Claydon, for championing this book from the initial hello. To my additional editors, Nancy Breen and Kelly Biscopink, who helped shape this book from beginning to end. Thank you also to the rest of the staff at F+W Media for their talent and attention to this project.

• Thank you to technical editor and stitch diagramist, Karen Manthey. The stitch diagrams are amazing and I'm so proud that we were able to include them.

• Thank you to all the fantastic yarn companies who generously supported this book and to the crochet industry for providing terrific products in great colors. Your colors and fibers inspire me. Your yarns have become my pets.

• Thank you to Tammy Hildebrand, who has become my sister in yarn. Your talent is surpassed only by your kindness and generosity.

• Thank you to Lisa Pflug, who was my first crochet friend in the CGOA and has continued to support me through both fair weather and hurricanes. I'm grateful for your help and friendship.

• There are so many others to thank who provided me with encouragement, chocolate, good wishes and opinions: Haley and Anna, my Ravelry group moderators; Missy and all my Jazzercise friends who didn't laugh at me as I crocheted before and after class and daydreamed about stitching during class; and the many, many blog readers who keep me company as I work from home.

• Thank you, God. I couldn't have done this book, or anything really, without you.

Table of Contents

Introduction

By now, you may have discovered the simple joy of working with a hook and yarn. Our time and money are precious though, so what's the best way to maximize our time and resources? Motif projects! Projects made of tiny units are the best for projects on the go.

Motifs are the ultimate in portability. The red centers in the *Trillions of Triangles* afghan were made while at a Cincinnati Reds' baseball game. A hook, scissors, a skein of yarn and the round 1 instructions were all that I needed to make a huge dent in this project. Many of these projects were made just this way: 10 minutes here, 15 minutes there, at soccer practice, in the waiting room of the doctor's office, riding in a car.

Motifs are magic because of how quickly they add up. I like to do mine assembly-line style. I do round 1 for all the motifs needed for the project, then go back and do round 2 for each motif. This way, I only have to take one color of yarn with me when on the go. Also, you can easily change the size of the project. If you get distracted or bored, just make a smaller blanket for a child or a pet. Have an extra-tall friend? Easily add more motifs to an average blanket to keep his feet warm. Add more motifs to make the blanket large enough for your bed. No one will know how big the project was supposed to be!

Motifs are also wonderful because you can play with the colors without much time and yarn commitment. Don't like it? It will only take a few minutes to whip up another one. And you can use motifs you don't love as coasters, doll-house rugs or (if they're cotton) dishcloths. Or, unravel it and measure how much yarn it took to crochet each round. Now you have valuable information when it comes time to buy your yarn or dig in your stash.

But even better than the portability and adaptability of motifs is the way crocheting small items can bring friends and families together. Most crocheters have learned the basic granny square at some point, and I am no exception. As a teenager, my Mom and I made a granny square blanket together for my grandmother. Choosing colors at random from the yarn stash, my mom and I had hours of fun holding them up to each other and saying, "What do you think of this one?" Mom joined the granny squares in cream yarn and made a simple edging. While Grandma enjoyed the blanket and its handmade uniqueness, it was the process of making the blanket together that I cherish most.

Soon you'll be as hooked on motifs as I am and will find yourself saying those famous last words, "I'll make just one more!"

Ready . . . Set . . . Go Crochet!

Someone once asked me, "Why do you have more than one hook?" to which I replied, "Does a painter have just one brush?" All humor aside, having the right tools is part of the fun of designing or stitching a great crochet project. Every crochet designer has favorite tools and basic techniques that help bring a new design to life.

As you work through the projects in this book, you'll discover the tools you like to work with, and soon you won't want to crochet without them!

The correct tools, quality materials and an understanding of the basic crochet stitches will arm you with the power to make beautiful crocheted projects and begin to design your own.

Fibers

Any of the projects or motifs in this book can be made with any smooth yarn. If you decide to design your own afghan, you will need to decide which fiber is right for your purposes.

TYPES OF FIBERS

There are so many beautiful yarn choices available that it may seem difficult to choose. For the blankets in this book, as with all projects, considering the function of the final product is critical to choosing the right yarn. How is the project going to be used? When designing afghans for this book, I have chosen acrylic, cotton, cotton blends, bamboo blends and wools.

I love acrylic yarn for its vast array of affordable colors. Acrylic is also durable and machine washable. In the past, some acrylic yarn was accused of being scratchy and uncomfortable. Right now, on beds in our house, we have some of the same yarns that are found in this book. We have washed and worn those blankets for years, and they have become softer and better draped from the first washing. If you prefer not to use acrylic, there are many other options for afghans.

Another option for crochet is cotton blend yarns. Cotton can be heavy (weighty) but is an excellent fiber. It is washable, natural and an excellent choice for warmer climates that don't need the thick warmth of wool.

Wool is a very warm option for afghans, but it requires a little more care in cleaning. Untreated wool can shrink and felt in the washing machine.

Superwash wool is really an ideal yarn for afghans. Though more expensive than acrylic, it is warmer and more natural.

There are many other fibers not used in this book that you can use if you like, such as alpaca, cashmere, rayon, linen, polyester and blends of all of the above.

YARN WEIGHT

Every type of fiber comes in every shape and weight: smooth, twisted, bouclé, thin to super bulky and everything in between.

Most yarns will have a weight identifier on its label. The weight system goes from 0 for lace weight yarns to 6 for super-bulky weight yarns. Most of the yarns in this book will be a 4 for worsted (medium weight) yarns. You can learn more about yarn weights on page 126.

Bumpy, bouclé, fuzzy, ribbon and other novelty yarns are not used in this book because they are not commonly used in afghans. As the designer, I chose yarns that would allow for crisp stitch definition. When you design your own afghan, you can use whichever yarn you want.

The Craft Yarn Council of America (www.craftyarncouncil.com) has a detailed explanation of this weight system, as well as many other informative lists about hooks, common measurements, standards and tips on how to read patterns and charts.

HANKS, BALLS, SKEINS AND DYE LOTS

Yarn comes wound in hanks, balls and skeins.

- **A hank of yarn** is wound into a larger circular shape and twisted; one end of the twist is then tucked into the other. "Hanked up" yarn will need to be untwisted and made into a usable ball before it can be stitched. If you do not have a yarn swift or ball winder, your local yarn shop will usually provide this service when you purchase the yarn.

- **A ball of yarn** is wound in a donut shape so that the working yarn pulls easily from the center after removing the yarn band label.

- **A skein of yarn** is wound in a much bigger ball. The dangling outer end of yarn is tucked into the bottom of the skein. The working end will pull from the middle of the opposite end. Some crochet projects tell you to use two strands of the same yarn held together. In this case, you can use both the working yarn from the center and the outer end of yarn simultaneously. Place the skein in a big bowl on the floor, so when it flops around it doesn't escape your reach.

- **A dye lot number** is a code placed on all yarn that is colored in batches. The dye lot will tell you if different hanks or skeins were dyed in the same batch, giving your project ultimate color cohesion. Make sure you purchase enough yarn in the same dye lot to complete your project.

11

Tools

HOOKS

Just like artist's brushes, crochet hooks come in all shapes and sizes. There are pointy hooks and flat hooks; there are gorgeous ornate wooden hooks, humble aluminum hooks and inexpensive plastic hooks; there are hooks with fat wooden or clay handles and hooks with egg-shaped ergonomic handles; there are even hooks that have batteries and light up!

Find a hook that is comfortable, one that you can grip without strangling. You might notice that plastic hooks "drag" a bit more through the yarn than aluminum hooks. Like some designers, you might love the warm feel of wooden hooks. When you design your afghan, you decide which tool to use…just be consistent within a project.

All hooks are not created equal. The diameter of the hook's shaft will be labeled either on the hook itself or on the packaging. All crochet hooks will feel slightly different, and you may crochet more loosely or tightly depending on the handle, even if the diameter is the same.

For these reasons, whichever hook you swatch and start your project with is the one you should stitch and finish your project with. If you can't remember, make a note, or take a digital photo of your hook with the swatch and yarn band so that you have a visual reminder of how you made the swatch.

Crochet hook sizes range from tiny steel hooks to much larger hooks. The larger the hook the larger the stitch will be. A hook is measured in millimeters (mm).

The letter or number of the hook may vary depending on the brand and country in which it was made, so the millimeter number is the most reliable method of identifying a hook. The projects in this book use 4 mm–8 mm hooks.

YARN NEEDLE

Whether you call it a yarn needle or a tapestry needle, it's an invaluable tool for weaving in ends. Some stitchers use a latch hook tool commonly used to make hooked rugs to weave in ends. The latch hook tool has a much bigger handle and is less likely to be lost in the couch. I use my bent tip yarn needles for weaving ends more than any other tool.

SCISSORS

While they may not be critical to the success of your project, you won't have a successful project without them! Scissors dedicated only to the cutting of fiber are the best. I have children's scissors in every toolbox and project bag, a basket by the bed, the coffee table, the office…you can never have too many scissors.

DIGITAL CAMERA

I couldn't design without my digital camera. I don't print out all the photos, but I use them as a visual reference to remind me of color placement, motif configurations, which hook I used, what stitch went where, earlier attempts before I ripped out and started again and many other details. And don't forget to share photos of your finished projects!

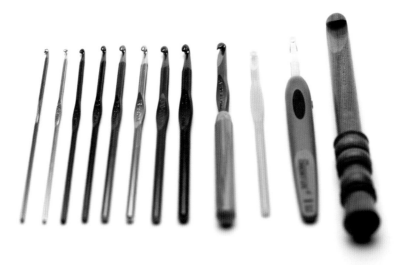

STITCH MARKERS

Stitch markers are handy in counting long foundation chains, counting edge stitches, marking the placement of stitches in crazy-to-see bouclé yarns and denoting the beginning of a round or pattern change. For this book, you will use a stitch marker to indicate the first stitch of a round. The stitch marker is then moved to the first stitch of the next round as work progresses. Stitch markers can be removed when the motif is complete or when stated in the pattern.

BLOCKING BOARD AND RUSTPROOF PINS

Blocking is a process of setting stitches in place either by wetting down or steaming the fabric and allowing it to dry to the desired measurements. Generally, stitchers only block natural fibers, though many people believe blocking acrylic yarns adds softness. To block a crocheted piece, pin the dampened piece to a foam mat with rustproof pins (because really, who wants rust stains on their yarn?) and allow the piece to dry. Blocking wires can hold bigger crocheted pieces with straight edges, but are not necessary for blocking the motifs in this book.

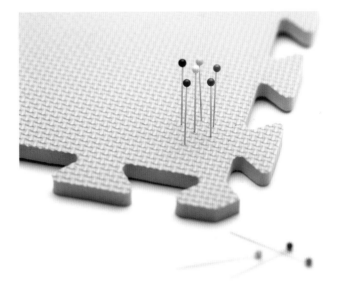

DESIGN KIT

If you are considering making your own original designs, I find that having a design kit handy is very useful.

In a gallon plastic zipper bag I keep:

- a pad of paper
- a pen
- scissors
- at least one skein of smooth worsted weight yarn
- at least one hook (appropriate for the yarn)
- at least one stitch marker

With just these things you can begin developing a design that is unique.

YOU!

Your hands and imagination are the best tools to bring to a project. Keep yourself in good condition by using good lighting and posture. Take breaks often and stretch to protect your joints from fatigue.

Larger handled hooks can ease tension in your hands and prevent strain. Your imagination is what will help you create your own original design, different from what anyone has ever seen before.

Using This Book

STITCH DIAGRAMS

Every motif in this book has both written word instructions and diagrammed symbol instructions. Each symbol in a stitch diagram represents one stitch.

When working a stitch diagram in the round, look to the center of the diagram and find the dot indicating the slip knot (which begins the work). The numbers in bold indicate the row or round number. Alternating rows or rounds are shown in different colors to help distinguish between them.

When looking at a symbol, the number of diagonal lines through the vertical part of the symbol indicates how many yarn overs are needed to complete the stitch. For example, the symbol for the treble crochet stitch has two diagonal hash marks across its vertical line indicating that it needs two yarn overs before beginning the stitch.

The most exciting benefit of a stitch diagram is that by comparing your motif to the diagram, it is immediately obvious whether you are on the right track or not. Because stitch diagrams are frequently used by crochet designers and publishers all over the world, a crocheter can easily transcend the language barrier and still complete projects written in other languages.

Refer to page 16 for a complete key of all the stitch symbols used in this book.

WRITTEN INSTRUCTIONS

Each instruction begins with the color of yarn, the size hook and the number of beginning chain stitches. Most of the motifs in the book will instruct you to form a ring to begin the first round.

Because the motifs are mostly symmetrical, we use an asterisk * to indicate the instruction that will be repeated. The instruction is given one time, then you are asked to repeat that instruction additional times to complete the round. At the end of the round, a total count of each type of stitch and space is given. Count stitches and check work before continuing to the next round.

Parentheses () are used to indicate that all the stitches within the parentheses should be put in the same stitch or space. For example: "(sc, hdc, ch 2, hdc, sc) in the next ch-3 sp" would mean to place all of those stitches, in that order, in the next ch-3 space. The difference between ch-3 and ch 3 is that the ch-3 has already been made and ch 3 is what you should do next. The dash makes all the difference.

If a set of instructions is still swimming before your eyes and it just doesn't seem to make sense, there are a couple things you can do:

- **Read** the instructions through before beginning.
- **Practice** new stitches on your swatch.
- **Compare** the instructions to the stitch diagram for clues.
- **Mark** your progress within a paragraph of instructions with a sticky note or flag.
- **Track** the number of times you repeat an instruction with a row counter tool.
- **Rewrite the instructions** with more space between steps. Place each phrase of the instruction on a new line and start a new line at every comma. Checkmark each step once you accomplish it.
- **Work assembly-line style** so you only have to memorize one or two rounds at a time. This will insure that each motif comes out the same. Even if you make a mistake, if it is consistent, it's likely no one will notice.

SKILL LEVELS

There is some discussion among crochet designers about the skill levels. The Craft Yarn Council of America created levels based on the competencies needed to complete a project:

- **Beginner Projects:** basic stitches, minimal shaping
- **Easy Projects:** basic stitches, repetitive stitch patterns, simple color changes, simple shaping and finishing
- **Intermediate Projects:** a variety of techniques, such as basic lace patterns or color patterns, mid-level shaping and finishing
- **Experienced Projects:** intricate stitch patterns, techniques and dimension, such as non-repeating patterns, multicolor techniques, fine threads, small hooks, detailed shaping and refined finishing

Many designers would rather describe how much focused concentration is needed to complete the project. Is it something that can be crocheted while watching the kids or does it need to be worked in complete quiet with no distractions?

Personally, I believe that anyone can complete any project given enough support and time. Crochet is not that physically difficult, but it may take some practice and instruction. But really, you can do it! It may take a little longer when you have to learn new stitches first, but I'm not asking you to do a 540 on a snowboard. If you make a mistake, you can just rip it out. It's just yarn!

GAUGE

Gauge is the number of stitches in an inch and the number of rows in an inch. Most patterns will present this information in terms of how many stitches are in 4 inches (10cm). It may read: 12 sts and 12 rows = 4" (10cm). That means in the given stitch pattern, if you take a hard ruler against your project, anywhere you measure, you should be able to count 12 sts in 4 inches (10cm) and 12 rows in 4 inches (10cm). If you are getting too many stitches per inch, you need to increase your hook size to create larger stitches. If you are getting too few stitches per inch, decrease your hook size to create smaller stitches.

For afghans, gauge is important because you don't want to run out of yarn—the bigger the stitches, the more yarn is used.

Gauge can also affect drape. If your stitches are too small and tight, the fabric is going to be dense, stiff and less drapey. Afghans want to be loose and casual, not tight and stiff.

For motifs and projects worked in the round, it is rare to measure gauge by the number of stitches and rows in an inch. However, more commonly, gauge will be measured in rounds.

A common measure of gauge in this book might read: Rnds 1–3 = 3" (8cm). That means, follow the pattern and at the end of round 3, the little piece should measure 3" (8cm) across. If your piece is larger than 3" (8cm), it is too big and you need a smaller hook. If it measures smaller than 3" (8cm), it is too small and you need a bigger hook.

I have designed the motifs in the book to all have an equal number of stitches. That doesn't mean that they will all measure the same number of inches. All the motifs' stitches will match up with one another, but you might have to do some playing with hooks so that any two motifs from the book will measure the same.

15

Stitch Glossary

Abbreviations, symbols and stitches you'll need to know:

∘ = chain (ch)

• or ▬ = slip st (sl st)

+ = single crochet (sc)

T = half double crochet (hdc)

T = double crochet (dc)

T = treble crochet (tr)

ʃ = front post half double crochet (FPhdc)

ʃ = front post double crochet (FPdc)

ʃ = back post double crochet (BPdc)

ʃ = front post treble crochet (FPtr)

+̃ = reverse single crochet (rev sc)

⋏ = single crochet decrease (sc2tog)

⋏ = single crochet three together (sc3tog)

∧ = double crochet decrease (dc2tog)

 = front post double crochet decrease (FPdc2tog)

 = front post treble crochet decrease (FPtr2tog)

 = front post double crochet three together (FPdc3tog)

 = cluster (cl)

 = beginning cluster (beg cl)

 = treble crochet cluster (tr-cl)

 = beginning treble crochet cluster (beg tr-cl)

 = popcorn (pop)

 = beginning popcorn (beg pop)

⌂ = picot

⌒ = worked through back loop (blp)

⌣ = worked through front loop (flp)

Slip Knot

Every crochet project begins with a slip knot on the hook.

With the index finger extended, pinch the cut end of the yarn between the thumb and middle finger up over the index finger. Wind the cut end around the thumb, and thread it under the index finger and behind the yarn loop. Put the cut end through the loop made by the thumb, withdraw the thumb and pull the cut end secure. Place the hook through the loop held by the index finger. Gently pull on the working end of the yarn to tighten the loop around the hook.

Yarn Over (yo)

Wrap the yarn around the hook, and grab the yarn with the hook. To yo more than one time, wrap the yarn around the hook the indicated number of times.

Slip Stitch (sl st)

Most commonly a slip stitch is used to join rounds or to advance the yarn to the next spot where it is more convenient.

Insert the hook in the indicated stitch or space, grab the yarn with the hook pulling it through both the stitch and the loop on the hook in one motion.

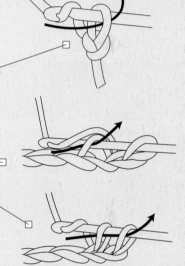

Chain (ch)

With a slip knot on the hook*, grab the working end of the yarn with the hook and pull through the loop on the hook. One chain made. Repeat from * as many times as instructed.

Single Crochet (sc)

Insert the hook into the next st, yo and pull up a loop through the stitch, yo and pull through both loops on the hook.

Reverse Single Crochet or Crab Stitch (rev sc)

Right-handed: Stitches are normally worked counterclockwise. To work in the reverse, go clockwise.

Left-handed: Stitches are normally worked clockwise. To work in the reverse, go counterclockwise.

Whichever hand you use, it's a little awkward to go the "wrong" way. Stitches are supposed to be somewhat lumpy and will look different. Follow the instructions for the single crochet but instead of inserting the hook in the next space or stitch as usual, go backwards a space or stitch and put the hook there. This is a great finishing edging.

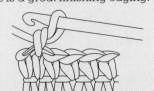

Half Double Crochet (hdc)

Yo, insert the hook into the next st, yo and pull up a loop through the stitch, yo and pull through all three loops on the hook.

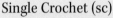
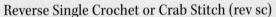

Double Crochet (dc)

Yo, insert the hook into the next st, yo and pull up a loop through the stitch, yo and pull through two loops on the hook, yo and pull through remaining two loops on the hook. You can see on the "post" of the stitch one diagonal wrap of yarn indicating that you yarned over once when you began the stitch. Now you can tell by looking at the stitch that it is a double crochet.

Treble (or Triple) Crochet (tr)

Yo twice, insert the hook into the next st, yo and pull up a loop through the stitch, yo and pull through two loops on the hook, yo and pull through two loops on the hook again, yo and pull through two loops on the hook a third time. You can see on the tall "post" of the stitch two diagonal wraps of yarn indicating that you yarned over twice when you began the stitch. Now you know can tell by looking at the stitch that it is a treble crochet.

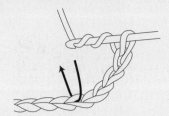

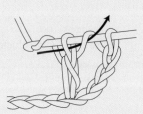

Double Treble Crochet (dtr)

Yo three times, insert the hook into the next st, yo and pull up a loop through the stitch, yo and pull through two loops on the hook, yo and pull through two loops on the hook again, yo and pull through two loops on the hook a third time, yo and pull through two loops on the hook a fourth time. You can see on the tall "post" of the stitch three diagonal wraps of yarn indicating that you yarned over three times when you began the stitch. Now you can tell by looking at the stitch that it is a double treble crochet.

POST STITCHES

All post stitches are made like regular stitches except for where you insert the hook at the beginning of the stitch. Usually, when you insert your hook to begin a stitch, the hook goes in the top two loops of the stitch beneath it. For any front post stitch, insert the hook from the front of the fabric that is currently facing you, around the post of the indicated stitch from right to left, yo and complete the stitch as usual.

For any stitch that is a back post stitch, insert the hook from the back of the fabric, around the post of the indicated stitch from right to left, yo and complete the stitch as usual. Post stitches can be decreased like regular stitches; the only difference is that the stitch is placed around the posts of the stitches below them instead of the top two loops of the stitch below.

Front Post Double Crochet (FPdc)

Yo, insert the hook from front to back around the post of the next stitch, yo and pull up a loop, (yo and pull through 2 loops on the hook) twice.

Back Post Double Crochet (BPdc)

Yo, insert the hook from back to front around the post of the next stitch, yo and pull up a loop, (yo and pull through 2 loops on the hook) twice.

Clusters are multiple stitches decreased down to one that were all placed in the same stitch or space. Later, we'll talk about decreased or together stitches, which are the same as clusters except each stitch is in its own stitch or space. Typically clusters are made of multiple double crochet stitches, although clusters can also be made of treble and double treble crochet stitches. A cluster can be any number of stitches, though it typically is an odd number: three, five or (more rarely) seven. If a pattern says cluster with no other explanation, it is assumed to be a cluster of three double crochets.

Cluster (cl)

(If no other explanation is given, it is assumed to be a cluster of three double crochets.)

Yo, insert the hook in the st or space (sp), yo and pull up a loop through the stitch, yo and pull through two loops on the hook, (half of the stitch now made), yo, insert the hook in the same st or sp, yo and pull up a loop through the stitch, yo and pull through two loops on the hook, (half of the second stitch now made), insert the hook in the same st or space, yo and pull up a loop through the stitch, yo and pull through two loops on the hook, (half of the third stitch now made), yo and pull through all four loops on the hook. One cluster is complete.

Beginning Cluster (beg-cl)

A beginning cluster is worked at the beginning of a round or row and a ch-3 is put in place of the first dc to get you started.

Ch 3 (counts as the first dc), yo, insert the hook in the same st or sp, yo and pull up a loop through the stitch, yo and pull through two loops on the hook, (half of the second stitch now made), insert the hook in the same st or space, yo and pull up a loop through the stitch, yo and pull through two loops on the hook, (half of the third stitch now made), yo and pull through all three loops on the hook. One beginning cluster is complete.

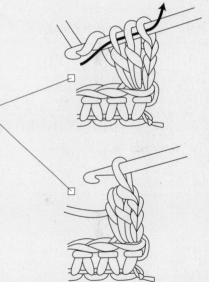

Treble Crochet Cluster (tr-cl)

*Yo twice, insert the hook in the st indicated, yo and pull up a loop, (yo and draw through two loops on the hook) twice; repeat from * two times more, yo and draw through all four loops on the hook.

Beginning Treble Crochet Cluster (beg tr-cl)

Ch 4 (counts as first tr), *yo twice, insert the hook in the sp indicated, yo and pull up a loop, (yo and draw through two loops on the hook) twice; repeat from * once more, yo and draw through all three loops on the hook.

Increasing is easy! You've probably already been doing it by accident. When more than one completed stitch goes in the same place, it is increasing the number of stitches in the row or round. Corners are examples of where stitches are increased. In many of the motifs in this book, a corner is made by placing three stitches into the corner space, increasing by two more than on the previous round. There is no specific abbreviation for increasing.

As explained in the cluster section, multiple stitches can be decreased or worked together into one. Sometimes you will see the abbreviation dc dec or dc2tog for two double crochets decreased into one. When you see dc dec, which is the traditional way of expressing a crochet decrease, decrease only one stitch. Dc3tog and Dc4tog are ways of decreasing three and four stitches respectively down to one. Similarly, other stitches can be decreased. Hdc2tog means to decrease two half double crochet stitches into one. Tr3tog means to decrease three treble crochet stitches into one. For the actual decreasing to happen, insert the hook to make the second half of the stitch in the next stitch or space…not in the same stitch or space like the cluster.

Single Crochet Decrease (Sc2tog)

(Insert the hook in the next st or space (sp), yo and pull up a loop through the stitch) twice, yo and pull through all 3 loops on the hook.

Double Crochet Decrease (Dc2tog)

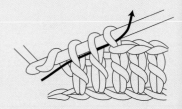

Yo, insert hook in the next st or space (sp), yo and pull up a loop through the stitch, yo and pull through two loops on the hook, (half of the stitch now made), yo, insert hook in the next st or sp, yo and pull up a loop through the stitch, yo and pull through two loops on the hook, (half of the second stitch now made), yo and pull through all three loops on the hook. Two dc are now one st, and the stitch count is decreased by one stitch.

Treble Crochet Decrease (Tr2tog)

(Yo twice, insert the hook in the next st, yo, pull through the st, yo, pull through 2 loops on the hook, yo and pull through 2 loops on the hook again) 2 times, yo, pull through all 3 loops on the hook. Two tr are now on st, and the stitch count is decreased by one stitch.

Triple Crochet Decrease (Tr3tog)

Yo twice, insert the hook in the next st or space (sp), yo and pull up a loop through the stitch, yo and pull through two loops on the hook, yo and pull through two loops on the hook again, (half of the stitch now made), yo twice, insert the hook in the next st or sp, yo and pull up a loop through the stitch, yo and pull through two loops on the hook, yo and pull through two loops on the hook again, (half of the second stitch now made), yo twice, insert the hook in the next st or space, yo and pull up a loop through the stitch, yo and pull through two loops on the hook, yo and pull through two loops on the hook again, (half of the third stitch now made), yo and pull through all four loops on the hook. Three treble crochets are now decreased to one stitch. The stitch count for the row or round has decreased by two stitches.

Most popcorn stitches are made with several complete stitches in one spot. After all the necessary stitches (usually 3 or 5 dc) are made in the same spot, they are tied together by removing the hook from the last st, insert-ing it in the top of the first st and also the top of the last st of the group, and pulling the working yarn through. This ties them into a neat package and makes them pop up from the surface of the fabric.

Popcorn Stitch (pop)

For the patterns in this book, the special stitches section will specify how to make the popcorn stitch needed for that pattern. Generally, popcorn stitches are multiple completed stitches of the same type in the same stitch or space. If the pattern calls for a 5-dc popcorn, then make a double crochet in the next st, then another in the same stitch, then another, until you have five completed double crochet stitches in the same stitch. Here's the tricky part… gently remove the hook from the one remaining loop, insert the empty hook in the top two loops of the first double crochet of the five you just made, grab the dangling abandoned loop, yo and pull through the loop now on the hook. Generally the instruction for a popcorn stitch is followed by a chain or two. Allow the jumble of five double crochets to pop forward off the surface of the project.

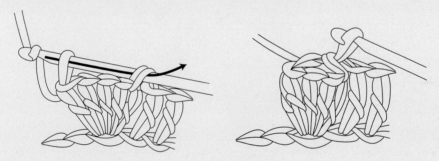

Beginning Popcorn (Beg-pop)

Using the example above, the first of the five double crochets is replaced with a traditional ch-3. This is used at the beginning of the row or round. Continue with the stitch by placing the remaining stitches in the same stitch or space and joining as described above. For a 5-dc beg-pop, you would work ch 3, 4 dc in same stitch, then proceed as with a regular popcorn.

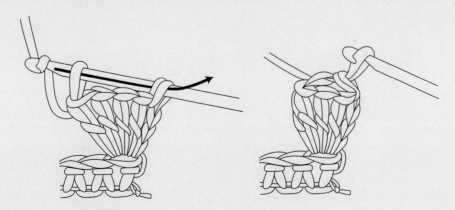

21

Creating Your Own Designs

Whether you want to design your own afghan for profit or for fun, the following pages will help you think through the decisions that will make it uniquely yours. After you work with my designs in this book, use these design ideas so you can start from scratch on your own projects.

WHY DEVIATE FROM THE PATTERNS?

Why not? I think of crocheting as playing—it's fun and it doesn't have to be expensive. Crochet is kind of like painting a room in your house—if you don't like it, you can repaint it. With crochet, if you don't like your yarn colors or making a particular motif, just choose another.

This is especially true when you are making an afghan for yourself because there are no rules. With garments, you have to try and choose a shape and color that are flattering to your body shape and type. But with an afghan, go ahead and choose yellow even if it doesn't complement your skin tone. Choose neon purple if you want! If you can find the yarn in the color you like, go for it.

Of course, many people love the structure of a pattern. After a stressful day of making choices that impact the health and future of our families, it's nice to just follow directions without question. There is much satisfaction, relaxation and benefit from stitching with a pattern. And you'll know you have found a great one when you make it again and again!

Being able to express yourself in crochet with color and shape is fun and might be the only chance you get to be creative in your day. You don't have to please anyone but yourself.

GOAL SETTING

When I set out to design, I start with various goals in mind:

• What will the project be?
• Where will it go?
• Who is it for?
• How will it be used?

The answers to these questions help me make the decisions that begin the project. If I am making a baby afghan for a shower gift, I might choose a different yarn than if I were choosing to make a blanket for a wedding gift. If I'm making a blanket for relatives who live in Minnesota, I'll choose a heavier yarn than for friends who live in Arizona.

Think back to your art appreciation classes in school. You probably discussed the concepts of repetition and variety, texture, unity, balance and symmetry. The same concepts apply in the flat canvas of an afghan. With that in mind, design your blanket to include:

• Repetition of stitches
• Color variation (either a little or a lot!)
• Spacing variation (a balance between holes and dense areas)
• Depth between foreground, middle ground, background

CHOOSING COLOR

Color is one of the first things we choose when making decisions for a design. I always consider the following:

- Where will the project go?
- Does it need to match someone's décor?
- What is the recipient's favorite colors?
- Does the yarn I want to use come in those colors?

Some of you probably have an innate sense of color, while others have to work at it. I have had to work at it, and I have a few tricks for you that I have learned along the way.

First, choose a main color that you definitely want and start there. The main color of your afghan can be the focal point. I like to then choose a color that will contrast in value with the main color. You can use a color wheel to help you find complementary colors to use in your blanket.

Let's say you choose purple for your main color. You could choose additional colors in any of the following schemes:

- **Complementary color scheme:** Choose the color that is opposite your main color on the color wheel (i.e., yellow)
- **Analogous color scheme:** Choose the colors that are next to your main color on the color wheel (i.e., red and blue)
- **Split-complementary color scheme:** Choose the colors that are next to the main color's complementary color (i.e., green and orange).

Choosing colors is one of the most fun parts of creating a project. I'd love to tell you to get out your color wheel and choose a color scheme from the color theories of renowned artists, but I can't. The truth is that not all yarn comes in every color. The good news is that the color wheel does have a huge amount of useful information that can guide you.

Complementary Colors

Analogous Colors

Split-Complementary Colors

COORDINATING COLORS

Using one main color can unify a scrap blanket. That color should go well with all of the scrap colors. Good choices for a unifying color might be cream, taupe, black, white, navy, gray or brown. The main color could be used for the joining, the edging and the middle of every motif.

Another way to unify the project when using many, many colors is to let all the colors be the same approximate value. When there is high contrast (different values), you can squint your eyes and let the colors blur, but still see the different sharp color changes. When all the colors are the same value, if you squint your eyes and let the colors blur, the colors all blend together.

Another easy trick for determining if colors go together is to take an 8 inch (20cm) strand of each color being considered, hold them all together and twist them together like a barber pole. Are they pleasing to look at when held together this way? Or does one stand out so it doesn't belong?

Another piece of good news is that the yarn companies have done much of the work for you. Often, the creative directors of yarn companies have worked very hard to choose colors that are trendy and go well together. If, however, you are one of the über-crafty people who spin or dye your own yarn, you can custom-make a color scheme. Most of us, though, are limited to the colors that are available through the yarn manufacturers.

Designers of fabric, papers and home décor have been doing much of the color research for us over the years. To find inspiration, look at fabrics and wrapping papers, items in nature and patterns on birds and animals. Look at the colors in home décor and fashion magazines, and advertisements. When looking to these things for inspiration also note the proportion of color on the paper of fabric. How much is each color represented? Is the color represented with a variety of shades of the same color?

Color preference is as different as each individual person. Most people just go with what they like. If you are unsure, swatch it up!

COLOR PLACEMENT

When choosing where colors will go in the motif, I either like to place the dominant color in the middle of the motif or make the dominant color the round in the motif that has the most texture—maybe even both! Place a lighter, less eye-catching color next to the dominant color so that they don't compete. In any project, the focus will be on:

• the very center of the project or motif
• the place where there is greatest contrast (where the lightest and darkest colors meet)
• where there is the most interesting texture

Emphasize textures by creating contrast near them and placing the dominant color in the textured areas.

LAYOUT OF MOTIFS

Motifs can be laid out in any configuration, but how do you determine this before you make hundreds of motifs and buy all the yarn? The answer is to buy one skein of each color you are considering. And then swatch, swatch, swatch! Make swatches in a variety of different color schemes. Then, take a digital photo of each one, filling the camera's frame with the entire swatch. With a few photo skills, copy and paste the photos next to each other in Adobe Photoshop or even Microsoft Word so you can imagine what the finished project might look like if the motifs were multiplied and placed together.

FILL-INS

After motifs are assembled together, some configurations of motifs might leave holes that need to be filled in with smaller motifs to complete the look. While working the last round of the fill-in motifs, join them to the finished project. The last round will be anchored to the motif itself and to its bigger neighbors, usually with a slip stitch or single crochet. Looking carefully at the motifs in the book, try to imagine them with just the first two or three rounds—they might be the right size and shape to act as fill-ins.

BUYING YARN

After you have swatched and perhaps played with the layout on the computer, you'll need to order or buy yarn. Because you figured out how many motifs you'll need and you have swatched and determined the yarn, you have all the information you need to buy the yarn.

Frog (rip-it rip-it) apart one of each of the motifs you are going to use. Measure how much yarn in yards is needed to complete each motif multiplied by the number of motifs needed to complete the project. Look at the number of yards that are in each skein and divide to see how many motifs can be worked from one skein of that color. Then, add one more skein of the color that will be used to assemble the motifs. Don't forget the edging! Do you have an edging in mind? Add a skein of each color that will be used in the edging rounds.

If you use multiple yarns in your project, make sure they are all the same fiber, requiring the same washing care. You may not want to mix wool and cotton within one blanket. In the wash, the wool would felt and the cotton might shrink a little. In other words, it could turn out all wonky!

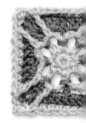

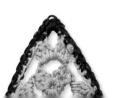

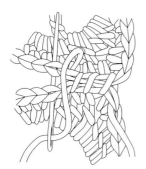

Whipstitch Join

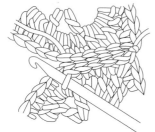

Sl St Join

SC (through 1 loop) Join

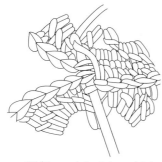

SC (through both loops) Join

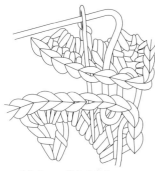

Mattress Stitch Join

ASSEMBLY

The method of assembly can move a blanket from average to extraordinary. There are several different standard methods, but you should feel free to invent your own.

- **Whipstitch:** Whipstitching is a very easy method of joining. You may recognize it as the looping running stitch that is common in sewing. With right or wrong sides facing, match up the stitches. With a yarn needle and a length of yarn of your choice, sew the motifs together. Sew either through the inner or outer loops only, or through both loops—you decide! Leave a tail dangling to weave in or sew over. Insert the needle from the back through the desired loops to the front of the sandwiched fabric. Allow the yarn to wrap around the edge as you bring the needle to the back, and pull through to the front again.

    When you whipstitch motifs together with the right sides facing each other and you sew through the outer loops only, you will see a ridge where the inner loops were not used. If the motifs are whipstitched with the wrong sides together through the outer loops only, the visible ridge will be on the back side of the blanket. If the motifs are whipstitched through both loops, there will not be a visible ridge.

- **Crochet:** Crocheting is the most fun way to assemble motifs. Use the same size hook as the project, and slip stitch or single crochet the motifs together. There is no reason, though, why you can't crochet a blanket together using a stitch pattern, reverse single crochet or another stitch. Make the stitches a design element by allowing the joining stitches to sit on the front of the blanket. Use a contrasting color to emphasize the shape of the motifs.

- **Join-as-you-go:** For those of you who dread assembling motifs, the join-as-you-go method is one of the best. To assemble in this way, the new motif is attached to previous motifs as the final round is worked. In this manner, each motif is joined as it is completed. If you prefer the assembly-line process of generating motifs, complete all the motifs except for the final round. Then, as the final rounds are all worked, they are joined together and voilà—you are done before you know it!

- **Mattress stitch:** In this method, lay the motifs flat open with either side up. With a yarn needle and chosen yarn, sew the motifs together by bumping the joined sides together.

EDGING

The edging on a blanket ties all the motifs together and frames the project. Like the frame on a painting, the edging can either complement and finish a project, or it can be distracting and eye-catching on its own. Even when following a book pattern, you can always change the edging if you wish, just like you can change the colors.

Because I love motifs and spend so much energy making them, I generally do not want an edge that will compete visually with what's inside. In the same way, I generally choose to let the unusual shaped edges of an octagon blanket to remain irregular, like in the *Reflected Sunlight* blanket. This allows the octagon shape to be preserved, even emphasized.

On some projects, the better choice might be to fill in the gaps along the edging with a half-motif to make a straight edge. It's your choice! A more ornate edging can be chosen, too. To create unity it's good to repeat the colors and stitches that were used in the motifs.

You may have seen how some quilters like to "break" the edging of their quilts and allow the design to reach into the binding, In the same way, I like my edgings to reach into the motifs. The *Blueberry Pancakes* project is an example of how this can be done.

Regardless of whether you choose an ornate edging or a simple one, I generally choose to do the first round of edging in the same color as the last row of the motif. This first foundation edging round helps even out the joins and create a smooth edge for the subsequent rounds. Also, if you made any mistakes, the first round of edging can help you smooth over any rough spots. Get the count right on the first round of edging and the rest will be smooth sailing.

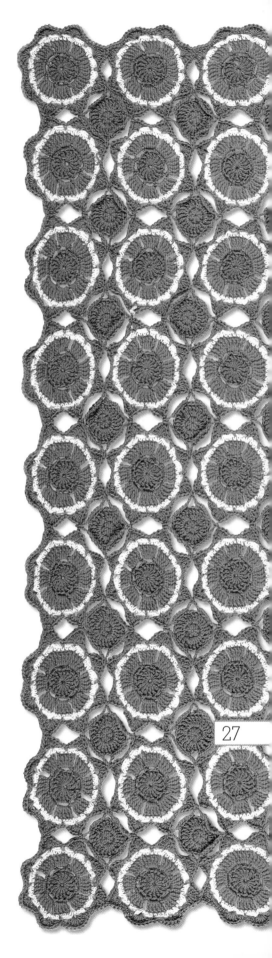

Motifs to Go

Motifs are portable, playful, convenient and perfect for those of us who like to stitch in unusual places—like at baseball games, on airplanes, in doctors' offices and before Jazzercise classes!

But the motifs in this book are extra-special because they are designed to mix and match with every other motif in the book. Each side of every triangle, square and hexagon has thirteen stitches (if you count the corners, which I do). The rectangles have thirteen stitches on the shorter sides and fifteen stitches on the longer sides. Some of the octagons have thirteen stitches on each side and others have irregular edges that are perfect for join-as-you-go projects.

Whichever combinations you choose, with a little finesse, they all can go together. Use these easily interchangeable motifs to devise or create your own fabulous projects. With this book, a little bit of time and your favorite yarns, you can build beautiful, lasting projects while you're on the go!

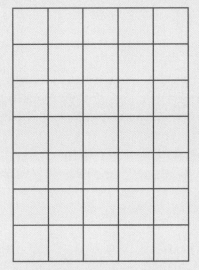

Side-by-Side Layout

Offset Brick Layout

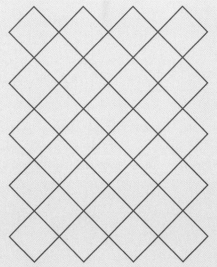

Diagonal Layout

SQUARES

Squares are important in crochet—they are truly the building blocks of many other shapes. If you can make a square, you can put many of them together to make purses, hats, sweaters, ponchos, blankets, coasters and scarves—the possibilities are limitless.

Squares are particularly appealing because they go together easily. They are logical and orderly, but they can also be wild and interesting. Put many of the same square motif together in one project, like in the *Flowers Galore* blanket, and they really make a statement! Change just one in a field of identical squares and the project takes on a whole new design interest. Offset them like bricks, leave the edges jagged or turn them on the diagonal, and the mood of the project changes.

Don't underestimate the design potential of a simple square!

Puddles Gather Rain
Skill level: Beginner | Finished measurement: 4" (10cm)

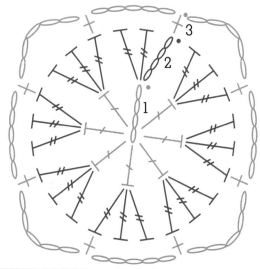

There is a lyric in a song called "No Rain" by Blind Melon about watching puddles gather rain. The design of this motif reminds me of that lovely lyric.

GETTING STARTED

YARN

• Worsted weight yarn in 2 different colors (A and B)

The motif shown at left was made using Universal Yarn Classic Worsted (80% Acrylic, 20% Wool, 3.5oz/100g balls/197yd/180m) in colors 7113 dazzling blue (A) and 637 light blue (B).

HOOK

• Size K/10½ (6.5mm) crochet hook or any size to obtain gauge

GAUGE

• Rounds 1–2 in pattern = 3" (8cm)

Motif

Note: All rounds are worked on the right side.

With color A, ch 4.

ROUND 1: 7 dc in 4th ch from hook; join with sl st in 4th ch of beg ch-4—8 dc. Fasten off.

ROUND 2: Join B with sl st in any st, ch 4 (counts as tr) 2 tr in same st; 3 tr in each of next 7 sts; join with sl st in top of beg ch-4—24 tr. Fasten off.

ROUND 3: Join A with sc in any st; *ch 5, sk 2 sts, sc in next st; rep from * 6 more times, ch 5; join with sl st in first sc—8 sc, 8 ch-5 sps. Fasten off.

Finishing

Weave in all ends.

Mix and Match with these motifs:

Flower Patch Motif

Purple Sunset Motif

Wrought Iron Motif

Acapulco Motif

Thumbprint Motif

Eyelets
Skill level: Intermediate | Finished measurement: 4½" (11cm)

When this motif is held up to the light, the petals of the flower are like eyelets in crisp, cotton fabric.

GETTING STARTED

YARN
- Worsted weight yarn in 2 different colors (A and B)

The motif shown at right was made using TLC Essentials (100% acrylic, 6oz/170g balls/312yd/285m) in colors 2220 butter (A) and 2680 eden green (B).

HOOK
- Size K/10½ (6.5mm) crochet hook or any size to obtain gauge

GAUGE
- Rounds 1–2 in pattern = 2½" (6cm)

Motif

Note: All rounds are worked on the right side.

With A, ch 5, join with sl st to form ring.

ROUND 1: Ch 1, 8 sc in ring; join with sl st in first sc, do not fasten off—8 sc.

ROUND 2: Ch 1, sc in same st; *ch 4, sc in next st; rep from * 6 more times; ch 4, sl st in first sc—8 sc, 8 ch-4 sps. Fasten off.

ROUND 3: Join B with sl st from back to front to back again around the post of any sc; ch 6 (counts as dc plus 3 chs); *BPdc around next sc, ch 3; rep from * 6 more times; join with sl st in 3rd ch of beg ch-6, do not fasten off—8 BPdc, 8 ch-3 sps.

ROUND 4: Ch 3, 2 dc in same st; *3 dc in next ch-3 sp, dc in next st, 3 dc in ch-3 sp**, 3 dc in next st; rep from * 2 more times; rep from * to ** once; join with sl st in top beg ch-3—40 dc. Fasten off.

ROUND 5: Join A with sc in middle dc of any 3-dc corner, 2 more sc in same st; *tr in ch-4 loop that is directly below in round 2, sk next st behind tr just made, sc in each of next 7 sts, tr in ch-4 loop directly below in round 2 **, sk st behind tr just made, 3 sc in next st; rep from * 2 more times; rep from * to ** once; join with sl st in first sc—8 tr, 40 sc. Fasten off.

Finishing

Weave in all ends.

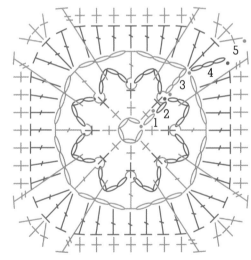

Mix and Match with these motifs:

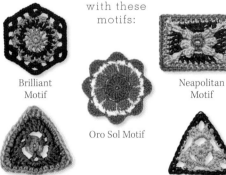

Brilliant Motif

Oro Sol Motif

Neapolitan Motif

Floating Triangle Motif

Whimsy Motif

33

Oscar Square
Skill level: Intermediate | Finished measurement: 4" (10cm)

As a child, I had a stuffed Oscar the Grouch toy that lived in an empty coffee can. I think that if Big Bird stood on his porch and looked down and to the right, this might be his view of Oscar in his garbage can.

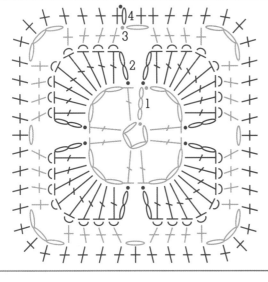

GETTING STARTED

YARN

- Worsted weight yarn in 2 different colors (A and B)

The motif shown at left was made using Bernat Satin (100% acrylic, 3.5oz/100g balls/163yd/149m) in colors 04221 soft fern (A) and 04203 teal (B).

HOOK

- Size K/10½ (6.5mm) crochet hook or any size to obtain gauge

GAUGE

- Rounds 1–2 in pattern = 3" (8cm)

SPECIAL STITCHES

- flp(s) = front loop(s) only
- blp(s) = back loop(s) only

Motif

Note: All rounds are worked on the right side.

With A, ch 4, join with sl st to form ring.

ROUND 1: Ch 3 (counts as dc), dc in ring, ch 3; *2 dc in ring, ch 3; rep from * 2 more times; join with sl st in top of beg ch-3, do not fasten off—8 dc and 4 ch-3 sps.

ROUND 2: Sl st in next st; *ch 2, 8 dc in ch-3 sp, ch 2, sl st in each of next 2 sts; rep from * 3 more times omitting last sl st; 32 dc, 8 sl st, and 8 ch-2 sps. Fasten off.

ROUND 3: Join B with sc in back loop only of first dc of any 8-dc group, sc in blp in next 3 sts, ch 3, sc in next 4 sts, skip sl sts and ch-sps; *ch 1, sc in blp in next 4 sts, ch 3, sc in blp in next 4 sts; rep from * 2 more times, ch 1, skip sl sts and ch-sps; join with sl st in first sc, do not fasten off—32 sc, 4 ch-1 sps, and 4 ch-3 sp.

ROUND 4: Ch 1, working in both loops of sts, sc in each of next 4 sts; *3 sc in ch-3 sp, sc in each of next 9 sts; rep from * 2 more times, 3 sc in ch-3 sp, sc in each of last 5 sts; join with sl st in top of first sc—48 sc. Fasten off.

Finishing

Weave in all ends.

Mix and Match with these motifs:

Cherry Cordial Motif

Scary Fun Motif

Twinkle Motif

Beveled Motif

Cameo Motif

Cherry Cordial
Skill level: Intermediate | Finished measurement: 4½" (11cm)

When I was little and had only a small allowance to buy gifts, I would buy boxes of chocolate covered cherries for my dad. Although I never cared for the candy, I always loved cherry cordial ice cream.

GETTING STARTED

YARN

• Worsted weight yarn in 2 different colors (A and B)

The motif shown at right was made using TLC Essentials (100% acrylic, 6oz/170g balls/312yd/285m) in color 2690 fusion (A) and Lion Brand Vanna's Choice (100% acrylic, 3½oz/100g balls/170yd/156m) in color 140 dusty rose (B).

HOOK

• Size K/10½ (6.5mm) crochet hook or any size to obtain gauge

GAUGE

• Rounds 1–2 in pattern = 2½" (6cm)

Motif

Note: All rounds are worked on the right side.

With A, ch 4, join with sl st to form ring.

ROUND 1: Ch 1, 8 sc in ring; join with sl st in first sc, do not fasten off—8 sc.

ROUND 2: Ch 3 (counts as dc), 2 dc in same st; *ch 4, sk 1 st, 3 dc in next st, rep from * 2 times, ch 4, sk 1 st; join with sl st in top beg ch-3—12 dc, 4 ch-4 sps. Fasten off.

ROUND 3: Join B with sl st in any ch-4 corner sp, beg-cl in same sp, (ch 2, cl) twice in same sp, ch 2; *sc in next 3 sts, ch 2, (cl, ch 2) 3 times in next ch-4 sp, rep from * 2 times, sc in last 3 sts, ch 2; join with sl st in top beg-cl—12 cl, 12 sc, 16 ch-2 sps. Fasten off.

ROUND 4: Join A with sc in middle cl of any 3-cl corner, 2 sc in same st; *2 sc in next ch-2 sp, sc in next cl, ch 3, sk next 2 ch-2 sps, sc in next cl, 2 sc in ch-2 sp**, 3 sc in next cl; rep from * 2 more times; rep from * to ** once; join with sl st in first sc—36 sc, 4 ch-3 sps. Fasten off.

Finishing

Weave in all ends.

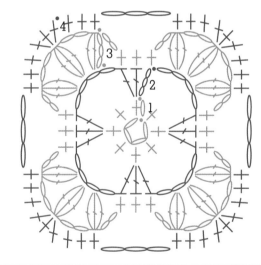

Mix and Match with these motifs:

Campfire Motif

Purple Pansy Motif

Harvest Motif

South Beach Motif

Beveled Motif

Flower Patch
Skill level: Intermediate | Finished measurement: 4¼" (11cm)

This motif looks like a flower, and a bunch together would look like a flower patch. This fun motif was named by our daughter, and it's bright and spunky, just like her!

GETTING STARTED

YARN
- Worsted weight yarn in 2 different colors (A and B)

The motif shown at left was made using TLC Essentials (100% acrylic, 6oz/170g balls/312yd/285m) in color 2820 robin egg (A) and Red Heart Super Saver (100% acrylic, 7oz/198g balls/364yd/333m) in color 256 carrot (B).

HOOK
- Size K/10½ (6.5mm) crochet hook or any size to obtain gauge

GAUGE
- Rounds 1-2 in pattern = 3½" (9cm)

SPECIAL STITCHES
- tr-cl = treble crochet cluster
- beg-tr cl = beginning treble crochet cluster

Motif

Note: All rounds are worked on the right side.

With A, ch 3, join with sl st to form ring.

ROUND 1: (Ch 4, sl st) 4 times in ring; join with sl st in first sl st—4 ch-4 sps, 4 sl sts. Fasten off.

ROUND 2: Join B with sl st in any ch-4 sp, (beg-tr cl, ch 3, tr-cl in same sp), ch 3; *(tr-cl, ch 3, tr-cl) in next ch-3 sp, ch 3; rep from * 2 more times; join with sl st in top of beg-cl—8 tr-cl, 8 ch-3 sps. Fasten off.

ROUND 3: Join A with sc in beg-cl where previously fastened off; *3 sc in ch-3 sp, sc in next cl, (2 sc, hdc, 2 sc) in next ch-3 sp**, sc in next cl; rep from * 2 more times; rep from * to ** once; join with sl st in first sc, do not fasten off—4 hdc, 36 sc.

ROUND 4: Ch 1, sc in same st, sc in next 6 sts; *3 sc in hdc, sc in next 9 sc; rep from * 2 more times, 3 sc in next hdc, sc in last 2 sts; join with sl st in first sc—48 sc. Fasten off.

Finishing

Weave in all ends.

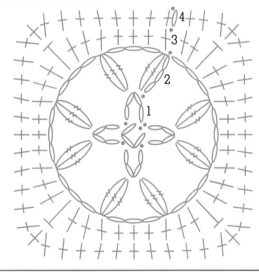

Mix and Match with these motifs:

Pick a Posie Motif

Last Blueberry Motif

Whimsy Motif

Vintage Motif

Octagon Medallion Motif

Chair Back
Skill level: Intermediate | Finished measurement: 3½" (9cm)

This motif reminds me of an elaborate chair back in antique furniture. It's a shout-out to my history of furniture professor. I still have the text as a coffee-table book.

GETTING STARTED

YARN
- Worsted weight yarn in 2 different colors (A and B)

The motif shown at right was made using Caron Simply Soft (100% acrylic, 6oz/170g balls/315yd/288m) in colors 9710 country blue (A) and 9726 soft yellow (B).

HOOK
- Size K/10½ (6.5mm) crochet hook or any size to obtain gauge

GAUGE
- Rounds 1–3 in pattern = 2¾" (7cm)

Motif

Note: All rounds are worked on the right side.

With A, ch 3, join with sl st to form ring.

ROUND 1: Ch 1, (sc, ch 5) 4 times in ring; join with sl st in top of first sc—4 ch-5 sps and 4 sc. Fasten off.

ROUND 2: Join B with sc in any ch-5 sp; *ch 2, dc2tog placing first leg in same ch-5 sp and 2nd leg in next ch-5 sp, ch 2**, sc in next ch-5 sp; rep from * 2 more times, rep from * to ** once; join with sl st in top of first sc, do not fasten off—4 sc, 4 dc2tog, 8 ch-2 sps.

ROUND 3: Ch 1, 3 sc in first st; *3 sc in next ch-2 sp, sc in next st, 3 sc in next ch-2 sp**, 3 sc in next st; rep from * 2 more times; rep from * to ** once; join with sl st in first sc—40 sc. Fasten off.

ROUND 4: Join A with sc where previously fastened off; *3 sc in next st, sc in next 9 sts; rep from * 2 more times, 3 sc in next st, sc in last 8 sts; join with sl st in first sc—48 sc. Fasten off.

Finishing

Weave in all ends.

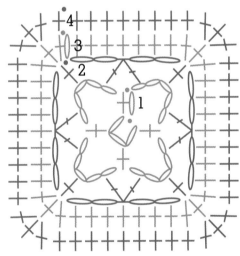

Mix and Match with these motifs:

Granny Octagon Motif

Neapolitan Motif

Serene Motif

Red Tide Motif

Flowery Day Motif

Pick a Posie
Skill level: Intermediate | Finished measurement: 4½" (11cm)

Bright and cheerful, this motif reminds me of one of my favorite flowers...the Gerbera daisy!

GETTING STARTED

YARN
- Worsted weight yarn in 2 different colors (A and B)

The motif shown at left was made using TLC Essentials (100% acrylic, 6oz/170g balls/312yd/285m) in color 2533 dark plum (A) and Red Heart Kids (100% acrylic, 5oz/141g balls/290yd/265m) in color 2846 cruise blue (B).

HOOK
- Size K/10½ (6.5mm) crochet hook or any size to obtain gauge

GAUGE
- Rounds 1–4 in pattern = 3½" (9cm)

Motif

Note: All rounds are worked on the right side.

With A, ch 4; join with sl st to form ring.

ROUND 1: Ch 1, 8 sc in ring; join with sl st in first sc—8 sc. Fasten off.

ROUND 2: Join B with sc in any st, sc in same st; 2 sc in each of next 7 sts; join with sl st in first sc—16 sc. Fasten off.

ROUND 3: Join A with sc in any st, ch 3; (sc, ch 3) in each of next 15 sts; join with sl st in first sc—16 sc, 16 ch-3 sps. Fasten off.

ROUND 4: Join B with sc in any sc, ch 4; *sc in next sc, ch 4, rep from * 14 more times; join with sl st in first sc—16 sc, 16 ch-4 sp. Fasten off.

ROUND 5: Working behind sts in round 4, join A with sc in any ch-3 sp of round 3; *ch 6, sk all sts on round 4, sk 3 ch-3 sps on round 3, sc in next ch-3 sp of round 3; rep from * 2 more times, ch 6; join with sl st in first sc, do not fasten off—4 sc, 4 ch-6 sps. Fasten off.

ROUND 6: Ch 3 (counts as dc) 2 dc in same st; *7 dc in next ch-6 sp, 3 dc in next st; rep from * 2 more times, 7 dc in next ch-6 sp; join with sl st in top of beg ch-3—40 dc. Fasten off.

ROUND 7: Join B with sc in middle dc of 3-dc corner, 2 sc in same st; *sc in next 9 sts, 3 sc in next st; rep from * 2 more times, sc in last 9 sts; join with sl st in first sc—48 sc. Fasten off.

Finishing

Weave in all ends.

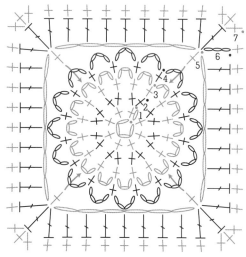

Mix and Match with these motifs:

Puddles Gather Rain Motif

Gift Package Motif

Off Center Motif

Red Light, Green Light Motif

South Beach Motif

Stain Berry
Skill level: Intermediate | Finished measurement: 4" (10cm)

This square is named for my favorite summer fruit salad made of strawberries, blueberries and red grapes.

GETTING STARTED

YARN

• Worsted weight yarn in 2 different colors (A and B)

The motif shown at right was made using Red Heart Super Saver (100% acrylic, 7oz/198g balls/364yd/333m) in color 528 medium purple (A) and Red Heart Eco-Ways (70% acrylic, 30% recycled polyester, 4oz/113g balls/186yd/170m) in color 1615 lichen (B).

HOOK

• Size K/10½ (6.5mm) crochet hook or any size to obtain gauge

GAUGE

• Round 1 in pattern = 2" (5cm)

Motif

Note: All rounds are worked on the right side.

With A, ch 4, join with sl st to form ring.

ROUND 1: Beg-cl in ring, ch 3, (cl, ch 3) 3 times in ring; join with sl st in top of beg-cl—4 cl and 4 ch-3 sps. Fasten off.

ROUND 2: Join B with sl st in any ch-3 sp; *ch 3, sl st in same sp, (sl st, ch 3, sl st) in next cl**, sl st in next ch-3 sp; rep from * 2 more times; rep from * to ** once; join with sl st in first sl st—8 ch-3 sps. Fasten off.

ROUND 3: Join A with sc in ch-3 sp over any cl; *ch 2, (2 dc, tr, 2 dc) in next ch-3 sp, ch 2**, sc in next ch-3 sp; rep from * 2 more times, rep from * to ** once, join with sl st in first sc, do not fasten off—4 sc, 8 dc, 4 tr, 8 ch-2 sps.

ROUND 4: Ch 1, sc in same st; *2 sc in ch-2 sp, sc in next 2 sts, 3 sc in next st, sc in next 2 sts, 2 sc in ch-2 sp**, sc in next st; rep from * 2 more times; rep from * to ** once; join with sl st in first sc—48 sc. Fasten off.

Finishing

Weave in all ends.

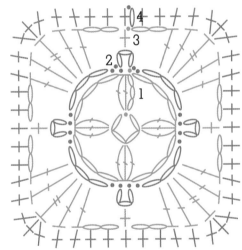

Mix and Match with these motifs:

Chair Back Motif

Hurricane Motif

Serene Motif

Purple Sunset Motif

Recycle Motif

Star Power

Skill level: Intermediate | Finished measurement: 4¼" (11cm)

Add dimension with this 3-D star. Imagine them all together, edge to edge, or combined with other motifs to provide movement. Spectacular!

GETTING STARTED

YARN

• Worsted weight yarn in 2 different colors (A and B)

The motif shown at left was made using Stitch Nation Alpaca Love (80% wool, 20% alpaca, 3oz/85g balls/132yd/121m) in colors 3920 ruby (A) and 3810 lake (B).

HOOK

• Size K/10½ (6.5mm) crochet hook or any size to obtain gauge

GAUGE

• Rounds 1–4 in pattern = 3" (8cm)

SPECIAL STITCHES

• flp(s) = front loop(s) only

• blp(s) = back loop(s) only

Motif

Note: All rounds are worked on the right side, unless otherwise stated.

WITH A, CH 4, JOIN WITH SL ST TO FORM RING.

ROUND 1: Ch 1, 8 sc in ring; join with sl st in flp of first sc, do not fasten off—8 sc.

ROUND 2: *Ch 6, sl st in 2nd ch from hook (point of star ray), sc in next ch, hdc in next ch, dc in each of next 2 ch, sl st in flp of next sc in round 1; rep from * 7 more times, join with sl st in first sl st—16 dc, 8 hdc, 8 sc. Fasten off.

ROUND 3: With WS facing, join B with sc in any unused blp of round 2, sc in next unused blp; *ch 3, sc in each of next 2 unused blps; rep from * 2 more times, ch 3; join with sl st in first sc, do not fasten off—8 sc, 4 ch-3 sps.

ROUND 4: Ch 3 (counts as dc), turn; (2 dc, ch 3, 2 dc) in ch-3 sp; *dc in each of next 2 sts (2 dc, ch 3, 2 dc) in ch-3 sp; rep from * 2 more times, dc in last st; join with sl st in top of beg ch-3, do not fasten off—24 dc, 4 ch-3 sps.

ROUND 5: Ch 3, do not turn, dc in each of next 2 sts, (2 dc in ch-3 sp, sc in point of star ray, 2 dc in same ch-3 sp); *dc in each of next 3 sts, sc in point of next star ray, dc in each of next 3 sts, (2 dc in ch-3 sp, sc in sl st point of next star ray, 2 dc in same ch-3 sp); rep from * 2 more times, dc in next 3 sts, sc in point of next star ray; join with sl st in top of beg ch-3—40 dc, 8 sc. Fasten off.

Finishing

Weave in all ends.

Mix and Match with these motifs:

Stain Berry Motif

Simplicity Motif

Oval in a Rectangle Motif

Rose Octagon Motif

Thumbprint Motif

Team Captain

Skill level: Advanced | Finished measurement: 5¼" (13cm)

Letterman jackets at Friday night football games, scarves and hats in school colors; this motif reminds me of all these things.

Motif

Note: All rounds are worked on the right side.

With A, ch 4; join with sl st to form ring.

ROUND 1: Ch 3, (counts as first dc), 13 dc in ring; join with sl st in top of beg ch-3, do not fasten off—14 dc.

ROUND 2: Ch 3, (counts as dc), dc in each of next 3 sts, ch 3, dc in next 3 sts, ch 3, dc in next 4 sts, ch 3, dc in last 3 sts, ch 3; join with sl st in top of beg ch-3—4 ch-3 sps, 14 dc. Fasten off.

ROUND 3: Join B with sl st in ch-3 sp before either 3-dc side, ch 3 (counts as dc) (dc in same sp, FPtr2tog around posts of dc before and after the ch-3 sp, 2 dc in same ch-3 sp), *dc in each of next 3 sts, 2 dc in next ch-3 sp, FPtr2tog around posts of dc before and after the ch-3 sp, 2 dc in same ch-3 sp, dc in next st, FPdc2tog around next 2 dc, dc in last dc of 4-dc side**, 2 dc in next ch-3 sp, FPtr2tog around posts of dc before and after the ch-3 sp, 2 dc in same ch-3 sp; rep from * to ** once; join with sl st in top of beg ch-3—4 FPtr2tog, 2 FPdc2tog, 26 dc. Fasten off.

ROUND 4: Join A with sl st in a FPtr2tog corner starting a side that does not have a FPdc2tog on it, ch 3 (counts as dc); *(FPdc around the FPtr2tog, dc in top of same st), dc in next 7 sts, (dc, FPdc, dc) in next st, dc in next 3 sts, FPdc around next st, dc in next 3 sts,** dc in next st; rep from * to ** once more; join with sl st in top of beg ch-3, do not fasten off—6 FPdc, 34 dc.

ROUND 5: Ch 1, sc in same st, 3 sc in next st; *sc in next 9 sts, 3 sc in next st; rep from * 2 more times, sc in each of last 8 sts; join with sl st in first sc—48 sc. Fasten off.

Finishing

Weave in all ends.

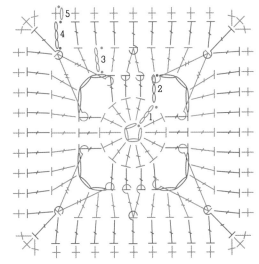

Mix and Match with these motifs:

Drama Queen Motif

South Beach Motif

Oscar Square Motif

Campfire Motif

Brilliant Motif

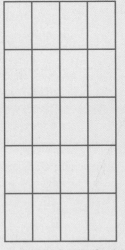

Vertical End-to-End Layout

Horizontal Layout

Bricks (with Squares) Layout

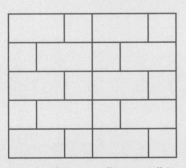

Paired with Squares (horizontal) Layout

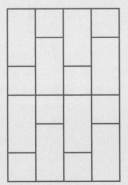

Paired with Squares (vertical) Layout

RECTANGLES

The crocheted rectangle motifs in this book are thirteen stitches wide by fifteen stitches long (if you count the corner stitches, which I do). You can stretch them into a more rectangular shape with blocking. With only a two-stitch difference between the sides, squares, triangles or hexagons can fit along the rectangle's short side. If you add a round to the square, triangle or hexagon and make them fifteen stitches on each side, they will fit along the longer side of the rectangles.

The instructions for stitching a rectangle can be a little more complicated than the instructions for the square. When joining new yarn, the instructions will specify that you are either to begin a short side or that you are starting a long side. Whether a right- or left-handed stitcher, yarn that is joined starting a short side will start in the indicated stitch when the first side worked is a short side. The short sides are the ones that have fewer stitches.

43

Vintage
Skill level: Beginner | Finished measurement: 3½" × 4" (9cm × 10cm)

Something about the lacy edge and the big flower in this motif reminds me of the cabbage rose. It harkens back to another time when glass-topped tables were covered to the floor with floral fabric.

GETTING STARTED

YARN

• Worsted weight yarn in 3 different colors (A, B and C)

The motif shown at left was made using Stitch Nation Alpaca Love (80% wool, 20% alpaca, 3oz/85g balls/132yd/121m) in colors 3810 lake (A), 3580 dusk (B) and 3620 fern (C).

HOOK

• Size K/10½ (6.5mm) crochet hook or any size to obtain gauge

GAUGE

• Rounds 1–2 in pattern = 2½" (6cm)

SPECIAL STITCHES

• blp(s) = back loop(s) only

• flp(s) = front loop(s) only

Motif

Note: All rounds are worked on the right side.

With A, ch 4, join with sl st to form ring.

ROUND 1: Ch 3 (counts as dc), 9 more dc in ring; join with sl st in top of beg ch-3, do not fasten off—10 dc.

ROUND 2: Ch 3 (counts as dc) working in blp of sts; dc in each of next 2 sts, ch 3, dc in each of next 2 sts, ch 3, dc in each of next 3 sts, ch 3, dc in each of next 2 sts, ch 3; join with sl st in top of beg ch-3—10 dc, 4 ch-3 sps. Fasten off.

ROUND 3: Join B with sc in a ch-3 sp beginning a long side (before a 3-dc side), 4 more sc in same sp, sc in each of next 3 sts, 5 sc in ch-3 sp, sc in each of next 2 sts, 5 sc in ch-3 sp, sc in each of next 3 sts, 5 sc in ch-3 sp, sc in each of next 2 sts; join with sl st in first sc—30 sc. Fasten off.

ROUND 4: Join C with sc in middle sc of sc-5 corner beginning a long side, ch 5, sc in same st; *[ch 3, sk 1 st, sc in next st] 3 times, ch 3, sk 1 st, (sc, ch 5, sc) in next st; ch 3, sk 2 sts, sc in next st, ch 3, sc in next st, ch 3, sk 2 sts**, (sc, ch 5, sc) in next st; rep from * to ** once; join with sl st in first sc—4 ch-5 sps, 14 ch-3 sps. Fasten off.

ROUND 5: (flower; not shown in diagram) Join A with sl st in any unused flp of round 1, ch 2 (counts as hdc), (hdc, ch 2, 2 hdc) in same st; (2 hdc, ch 2, 2 hdc) in each of the next 9 unused flp; join with sl st in top beg ch-2—40 hdc, 10 ch-2 sps. Fasten off.

Finishing

Weave in all ends.

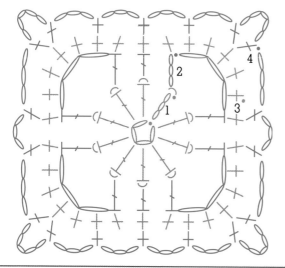

Mix and Match with these motifs:

Purple Sunset Motif

Beveled Motif

Flowery Day Motif

Oscar Square Motif

Puddles Gather Rain Motif

Thumbprint

Skill level: Easy | Finished measurement: 4¼" × 5" (11cm × 13cm)

This motif looks like an ink-pad thumbprint. Did you ever make pictures out of your fingerprints as a child, adding eyes and moustaches, hats, arms and legs to the little fingerprint body? Too cute!

GETTING STARTED

YARN
- Worsted weight yarn in 4 different colors (A, B, C and D)

The motif shown at right was made using Spud & Chloe, Sweater (55% super-wash wool, 45% organic cotton, 3.5oz/100g hanks/160yd/146m) in colors 7505 firefly (A), 7504 lake (B), 7506 toast (C) and 7509 firecracker (D).

HOOK
- Size K/10½ (6.5mm) crochet hook or any size to obtain gauge

GAUGE
- Rounds 1–2 in pattern = 2" × 3" (5cm × 8cm)

Motif

Note: All rounds are worked on the right side.

ROUND 1: With A, ch 8, 5 dc in 4th ch from hook, (the first 3 chs from hook compose a dc), dc in next 3 ch, 6 dc in last ch; working along unused foundation of chs, dc in next 3 ch sts; join with sl st in top of beg ch-3—18 dc. Fasten off.

ROUND 2: Join B with sc where previously fastened off, sc in same st, 2 sc in each of next 5 sts, sc in next 3 sts, 2 sc in each of next 6 sts, sc in last 3 sts; join with sl st in first sc—30 sc. Fasten off.

ROUND 3: Join C with sc in st where previously fastened off, ch 4, sk 3 sts, sc in next 2 sts, ch 1, sc in next 2 sts, ch 4, sk 3 sts, sc in next 5 sts, ch 4, sk 3 sts, sc in next 2 sts, ch 1, sc in next 2 sts, ch 4, sk 3 sts, sc in last 4 sts; join with sl st in first sc—18 sc, 2 ch-1 sps, 4 ch-4 sps. Fasten off.

ROUND 4: Join D with sl st where previously fastened off, ch 3 (counts as dc), (3 dc, tr, 2 dc) in ch-4 sp, dc in next 5 sts (including the ch-1 sp), (2 dc, tr, 3 dc) in next ch-4 sp, dc in next 5 sts, (3 dc, tr, 2 dc) in ch-4 sp, dc in next 5 sts (including the ch-1 sp), (2 dc, tr, 3 dc) in ch-4 sp, dc in last 4 sts; join with sl st in top of beg ch-3, do not fasten off—4 tr, 40 dc.

ROUND 5: Ch 1, sc in same st, sc in next 3 sts, 3 sc in next st, sc in next 9 sts, 3 sc in next st, sc in next 11 sts, 3 sc in next st, sc in next 9 sts, 3 sc in next st, sc in last 7 sts; join with sl st in first sc—52 sc. Fasten off.

Finishing

Weave in all ends.

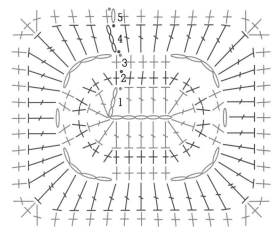

Mix and Match with these motifs:

Chair Back Motif

Whimsy Motif

Rose Octagon Motif

Red Light, Green Light Motif

Pick a Posie Motif

Polka Dot
Skill level: Easy | Finished measurement: 4½" × 5" (11cm × 13cm)

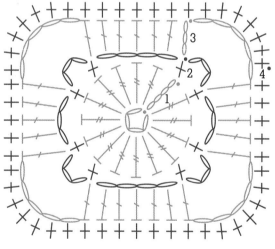

Put many of these little rectangles together and get one great optical illusion. Make it in black and white, or red and white, for a great retro style.

GETTING STARTED

YARN
- Worsted weight yarn in 2 different colors (A and B)

The motif shown at left was made using Lion Brand Vanna's Choice (100% acrylic, 3.5oz/100g balls/170yd/156m) in colors 144 magenta (A) and 099 linen (B).

HOOK
- Size K/10½ (6.5mm) crochet hook or any size to obtain gauge

GAUGE
- Round 1 in pattern = 2½" (6cm)

Motif

Note: All rounds are worked on the right side.

With A, ch 4, join with sl st to form ring.

ROUND 1: Ch 4 (counts as tr), 15 tr in ring; join with sl st in top beg ch-4—16 tr. Fasten off.

ROUND 2: Join B with sc in any st, ch 4, sk 3 sts, sc in next st, ch 3, sc in next st, ch 3, sk 1 st, sc in next st, ch 3, sc in next st, ch 4, sk 3 sts, sc in next st, ch 3, sc in next st, ch 3, sk 1 st, sc in next st, ch 3; join with sl st in first st, do not fasten off—8 sc, 2 ch-4 sps, 6 ch-3 sps.

ROUND 3: Ch 3 (counts as dc); *5 dc in ch-4 sp, dc in next st, ch 5, sk ch-3 sp, dc in next st, 3 dc in ch-3 sp, dc in next st, ch 5**, sk ch-3 sp, dc in next st; rep from * to ** once; join with sl st in top of beg ch-3—24 dc, 4 ch-5 corner sps. Fasten off.

ROUND 4: Join A with sc in ch-5 corner sp before the fasten off, 6 sc in same sp; *sc in each of next 7 sts, 7 sc in ch-5 sp, sc in each of next 5 sts**, 7 sc in ch-5 sp; rep from * to ** once; join with sl st in first sc—52 sc. Fasten off.

Finishing

Weave in all ends.

Beveled Motif

Red Tide Motif

Mix and Match with these motifs:

Stain Berry Motif

Serene Motif

Raspberry Tart Motif

Oval in a Rectangle
Skill level: Easy | Finished measurement: 4¼" × 5¼" (11cm × 13cm)

There just aren't enough ovals in crochet. I love the oval, and I hope you'll learn to love it, too.

GETTING STARTED

YARN

• Worsted weight yarn in 3 different colors (A, B and C)

The motif shown at right was made using Stitch Nation Bamboo Ewe (55% viscose from bamboo, 45% wool, 3.5oz/100g balls/177yd/162m) in colors 5830 periwinkle (A), 5510 beach glass (B) and 5875 twilight (C).

HOOK

• Size K/10½ (6.5mm) crochet hook or any size to obtain gauge

GAUGE

• Rounds 1–2 in pattern = 2½" × 3¼" (6cm × 8cm)

SPECIAL STITCHES

• blp(s) = back loop(s) only

Motif

Note: All rounds are worked on the right side.

With A, ch 8

ROUND 1: 5 dc in the 4th ch from hook, dc in each of next 3 chs, 6 dc in last ch, now working along foundation, dc in each of next 3 chs; join with sl st in top of first 3 chs, do not fasten off—18 dc.

ROUND 2: Ch 3 (counts as dc), dc in same st, 2 dc in each of next 5 sts, ch 2, sk 3 dc, 2 dc in each of next 6 sts, ch 2, sk 3 dc; join with sl st in top of beg ch-3—24 dc, 2 ch-2 sps. Fasten off.

ROUND 3: Join B with sl st where previously fastened off, ch 3 (counts as dc), dc in same st, dc in next st; *dc in next st, 2 dc in next st**; rep from * to ** 4 more times, ch 2, sk ch-2 sp, 2 dc in next st, dc in next st; rep from * to ** 5 more times, ch 2, sk ch-2 sp; join with sl st in top beg ch-3—36 dc, 2 ch-2 sps. Fasten off.

ROUND 4: Working in blps only; join C with sc in either ch-2 sp, 2 sc in same sp; *sc in each of next 2 sts, hdc in next st, dc in next st, (dc, tr, dc) in next st, dc in next st, hdc in next st, sc in each of next 2 sts, ch 1, sc in each of next 2 sts, hdc in next st, dc in next st, (dc, tr, dc) in next st, dc in next st, hdc in next st, sc in each of next 2 sts**; 3 sc in ch-2 sp; rep from * to ** 1 more time; join with sl st in first sc—4 tr, 16 dc, 8 hdc, 22 sc, 2 ch-1 sps. Fasten off.

Finishing

Weave in all ends.

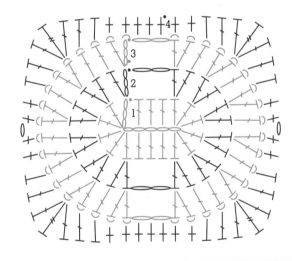

Mix and Match with these motifs:

Campfire Motif

Granny Octagon Motif

Stain Berry Motif

Chair Back Motif

Floating Triangle Motif

Last Blueberry

Skill level: Easy

Finished measurement: 4½" × 5" (11cm × 13cm)

Blueberry pancakes or blueberries plain—it doesn't matter because we love blueberries! This motif is a one-act play of four arms reaching for the last blueberry.

▌ G E T T I N G   S T A R T E D

YARN

- Worsted weight yarn in 3 different colors (A, B and C)

The motif shown at left was made using Red Heart Super Saver (100% acrylic, 7oz/198g balls/364yd/333m) in color 385 royal (A); Red Heart Kids (100% acrylic, 5oz/140g balls/290yd/265m) in color 2650 pistachio (B); TLC Essentials (100% acrylic, 6oz/170g balls/312yd/285m) in color 2690 fusion (C).

HOOK

- Size K/10½ (6.5mm) crochet hook or any size to obtain gauge

GAUGE

- Rounds 1–2 in pattern = 3" × 3½" (8cm × 9cm)

SPECIAL STITCHES

- blp(s) = back loop(s) only

Motif

Note: All rounds are worked on the right side.

With A, ch 6, join with sl st to form ring.

ROUND 1: Beg-cl in ring, ch 3, (cl, ch 3) in ring; (cl, ch 2), in ring, (cl, ch 3) 2 times in ring, (cl, ch 2) in ring; join with sl st in top of beg-cl—6 cl, 4 ch-3 sps, 2 ch-2 sps. Fasten off.

ROUND 2: Join B with sl st in any ch-3 sp before a ch-2 sp, (beg-cl, ch 3, cl) in same sp, ch 1, cl in next ch-2 sp, ch 1, (cl, ch 3, cl) in next ch-3 sp, ch 1, (cl, ch 3, cl) in next ch-3 sp, ch 1, cl in next ch-2 sp, ch 1, (cl, ch 3, cl) in next ch-3 sp, ch 1; join with sl st in top beg-cl—10 cl, 4 ch-3 sps, 6 ch-1 sps. Fasten off.

ROUND 3: Join C with sc in ch-3 sp before a long side (with 2 ch-1 sps), (sc, dtr between clusters of round 1 into beg ch-6 ring, 2 sc) in same sp; *sc in next cl, [2 sc in next ch-1 sp, sc in next cl] twice, (2 sc, dtr between clusters of round 1 into beg ch-6 ring, 2 sc) in next ch-3 sp, 2 sc in next cl, sc in ch-1 sp, 2 sc in next cl**; (2 sc, dtr between clusters of round 1 into beg ch-6 ring, 2 sc) in next ch-3 sp; rep from * to ** once; join with sl st in first sc—4 dtr, 40 sc. Fasten off.

ROUND 4: Working in blps only; join A with sc in dtr of a corner before either long side, 2 more sc in same st, sc in each of next 11 sts, 3 sc in next st, sc in next 9 sts, 3 sc in next st, sc in next 11 sts, 3 sc in next st, sc in next 9 sts; join with sl st in first sc—52 sc. Fasten off.

Finishing

Weave in all ends.

Mix and Match with these motifs:

Acapulco Motif

Puddles Gather Rain Motif

Cherry Cordial Motif

Twinkle Motif

Oro Sol Motif

Inspired by the Art Deco style of the buildings in Miami, Florida, imagine this little rectangle in stucco.

South Beach

Skill level: Intermediate

Finished measurement: 4¼" × 5¼" (11cm × 13cm)

GETTING STARTED

YARN
• Worsted weight yarn in 3 different colors (A, B and C)

The motif shown at right was made using Red Heart Kids (100% acrylic, 5oz/141g balls/290yd/265m) in colors 2650 pistachio (A) and 2846 cruise blue (C); TLC Essentials (100% acrylic, 6oz/170g balls/312yd/285m) in color 2500 teal (B).

HOOK
• Size K/10½ (6.5mm) crochet hook or any size to obtain gauge

GAUGE
• Rounds 1–3 in pattern = 2¾" × 3" (7cm × 8cm)

Motif

Note: All rounds are worked on the right side.

With A, ch 6; join with sl st to form ring.

ROUND 1: Ch 1, sc in ring, ch 2, 3 sc in ring, ch 2, sc in ring, ch 2, 3 sc in ring, ch 2; join with sl st in first sc—8 sc, 4 ch-2 sps. Fasten off.

ROUND 2: Join B with sl st in the single sc where fastened off, ch 3 (counts as dc), 3 dc in ch-2 sp, dc in next 3 sts, 3 dc in next ch-2 sp, dc in next st, 3 dc in next ch-2 sp, dc in next 3 sts, 3 dc in next ch-2 sp; join with sl st in top of beg ch-3—20 dc. Fasten off.

ROUND 3: Join C with sc in middle dc of 3-dc corner before either short side, 2 sc in same st, sc in next 3 sts, 3 sc in next st, sc in next 5 sts, 3 sc in next st, sc in next 3 sts, 3 sc in next st, sc in last 5 sts; join with sl st in first sc—28 sc. Fasten off.

ROUND 4: Join B with sc in middle sc in 3-sc corner before either short side, ch 3, sc in same st; *sc in next st, ch 3, sk next 3 sts, sc in next st, (sc, ch 3, sc) in next st, sc in next st, ch 3, sk next 2 sts, sc in next st, ch 3, sk next 2 sts, sc in next st**, (sc, ch 3, sc) in next st; rep from * to ** once; join with sl st in first sc—18 sc, 10 ch-3 sps. Fasten off.

ROUND 5: Join A with sl st in ch-3 corner sp before either short side, ch 3 (counts as dc), 6 dc in same sp; *sk next 2 sts, working behind ch-3 sp and working into skipped sts of round 3, dc in each of next 3 sts, sk next 2 sts on round 4, 7 dc in next ch-3 corner sp, sk next 2 sts, working behind ch-3 sp, dc in 2 skipped sts of round 3, hdc in next sc in round 4, working behind ch-3 sp, dc in 2 skipped sts of round 3, sk next 2 sts**, 7 dc in ch-3 corner; rep from * to ** once; join with sl st in top of beg ch-3—2 hdc, 42 dc. Fasten off.

ROUND 6: Join C with sc in middle dc of any 7-dc corner before a short side, 2 sc in same st, sc in next 9 sts, 3 sc in next st, sc in next 11 sts, 3 sc in next st, sc in next 9 sts, 3 sc in next st, sc in last 11 sts; join with sl st in first sc—52 sc. Fasten off.

Finishing

Weave in all ends.

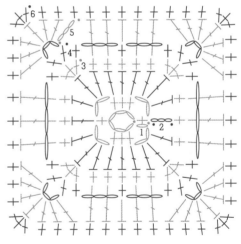

Mix and Match with these motifs:

Oscar Square Motif

Drama Queen Motif

Simplicity Motif

Golden Hexagon Motif

Flower Patch Motif

Cameo

Skill level: Intermediate | Finished measurement: 5" × 5½" (13cm × 14cm)

Like a modern interpretation of a traditional Victorian cameo, this little gem is lovely surprise.

GETTING STARTED

YARN

• Worsted weight yarn in 2 different colors (A and B)

The motif shown at left was made using Stitch Nation Alpaca Love (80% wool, 20% alpaca, 3oz/85g balls/132yd/121m) in colors 3620 fern (A) and 3580 dusk (B).

HOOK

• Size K/10½ (6.5mm) crochet hook or any size to obtain gauge

GAUGE

• Rounds 1–2 in pattern = 2½" × 3" (6cm × 8cm)

Motif

Note: All rounds are worked on the right side.

With A, ch 4, join with sl st to form ring.

ROUND 1: Ch 3 (counts as dc) 11 dc in ring; join with sl st in top of beg ch-3, do not fasten off—12 dc.

ROUND 2: *Ch 4, sk next 2 dc, 5 dc in next st, ch 4, sk next 2 sts, sc in next dc; rep from * 1 more time; join with sl st in ch-4 sp—10 dc, 4 ch-4 sps, 2 sc. Fasten off.

ROUND 3: Join B with sl st in ch-4 sp where previously fastened off, ch 3 (counts as dc) 4 more dc in same sp; *ch 2, sk next 2 sts, sc in next st, ch 2, sk next 2 sts, 5 dc in next ch-4 sp; ch 3**, 5 dc in ch-4 sp; rep from * to ** once; join with sl st in top of beg ch-3—20 dc, 2 ch-3 sps, 4 ch-2 sps, 2 sc. Fasten off.

ROUND 4: Join A with sc in same st as previously fastened off, sc in next 4 dc; *sc in next ch-2 sp, FPdc around 2nd dc of 5-dc group on round 3, sc in same ch-2 sp in current round, sc in next sc, sc in next ch-2 sp, FPdc around 4th dc of 5-dc group on round 3, sc in same ch-2 sp in current round, sc in each of next 5 dc, 5 sc in next ch-3 sp, ** sc in each of next 5 dc; rep from * to ** once; join with sl st in first sc—40 sc, 4 FPdc. Fasten off.

ROUND 5: Join B with sc in st where previously fastened off, ch 4 (counts as dc plus ch 1); sk 1 sc; *tr in next st, ch 1, sk 1 st, dc in next st, hdc in next st, sc in each of next 5 sts, hdc in next st, dc in next st, ch 1, sk 1 st, tr in next st; ch 1, sk 1 st, dc in next st, hdc in next st, sc in each of next 3 sts, hdc in next st**, dc in next st, ch 1, sk 1 st; rep from * to ** once; join with sl st in 3rd ch of beg ch-4, do not fasten off—4 tr, 8 dc, 8 hdc, 16 sc.

ROUND 6: Ch 1, sc in same st; *sc in next ch-1 sp, 3 sc in next st, sc in next ch-1 sp, sc in each of next 9 sts, sc in ch-1 sp, 3 sc in next st, sc in next ch-1 sp**, sc in each of next 7 sts; rep from * to ** once, sc in next 6 sts; join with sl st in first sc—52 sc. Fasten off.

Finishing

Weave in all ends.

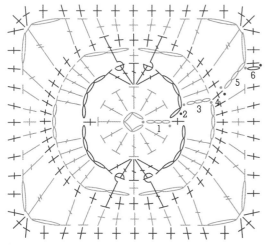

Mix and Match with these motifs:

Floral Octagon Motif

Flower Patch Motif

Campfire Motif

Recycle Motif

Bluebonnet Motif

Neapolitan

Skill level: Intermediate | Finished measurement: 4" × 4½" (10cm × 11cm)

There is a cute car called a Metropolitan that I always loved. If it was pink with a brown interior, it could be a Neapolitan Metropolitan!

GETTING STARTED

YARN

• Worsted weight yarn in 3 different colors (A, B and C)

The motif shown at right was made using Red Heart Eco-Ways (70% acrylic, 30% recycled polyester, 4oz/113g balls/186yd/170m) in colors 3374 rose dust (A), 3372 petal (B) and 3344 bark (C).

HOOK

• Size K/10½ (6.5mm) crochet hook or any size to obtain gauge

GAUGE

• Rounds 1–2 in pattern = 2" × 2½" (5cm × 6cm)

SPECIAL STITCHES

• beg pop = beginning popcorn

• pop = popcorn (5 dc)

• FPtr = Front Post treble crochet

Motif

Note: All rounds are worked on the right side.

With A, ch 5, join with sl st to form ring.

ROUND 1: Ch 3 (counts as dc), 9 dc in ring; join with sl st in top of beg ch-3—10 dc. Fasten off.

ROUND 2: Join B with sl st in any dc, beg pop in first st, ch 2; pop in next st, ch 2, pop in next st, ch 5, sk 2 sts, pop in next st, ch 2, pop in next st, ch 2, pop in next st, ch 5, sk 2 sts; join with sl st in top of first pop—6 pop, 4 ch-2 sps, 2 ch-5 sps. Fasten off.

ROUND 3: Join C with sl st in either ch-5 sp, ch 3 (counts as dc), 4 dc in same sp, dc in next st, ch 3, 2 dc in ch-2 sp, dc in next st, 2 dc in ch-2 sp, ch 3, dc in next st, 5 dc in ch-5 sp, dc in next st, ch 3, 2 dc in ch-2 sp, dc in next st, 2 dc in ch-2 sp, ch 3, dc in next st; join with sl st in top beg ch-3—24 dc, 4 ch-3 sps. Fasten off.

ROUND 4: Join B with sc in the first dc of a long side, sc in each of next 6 sts, (2 sc, FPtr around join of pop, 2 sc) in next ch-3 sp, sc in each of next 5 sts, (2 sc, FPtr around join of pop, 2 sc) in next ch-3 sp, sc in each of next 7 sts, (2 sc, FPtr, 2 sc) in next ch-3 sp, sc in each of next 5 sts, (2 sc, FPtr, 2 sc) in next ch-3 sp; join with sl st in first sc—4 FPtr, 40 sc. Fasten off.

ROUND 5: Join A with sc in FPtr beginning a long side, 2 sc in same st, sc in each of next 11 sts, 3 sc in next st, sc in each of next 9 sts, 3 sc in next st, sc in each of next 11 sts, 3 sc in next st, sc in each of last 9 sts; join with sl st in first sc—52 sc. Fasten off.

Finishing

Weave in all ends.

Mix and Match with these motifs:

Octagon Medallion Motif

Star Power Motif

Acapulco Motif

Eyelets Motif

Harvest Motif

Scary Fun
Skill level: Intermediate
Finished measurement: 5" × 5½" (13cm × 14cm)

I'm not sure when green and purple entered the Halloween color scheme, but I like it!

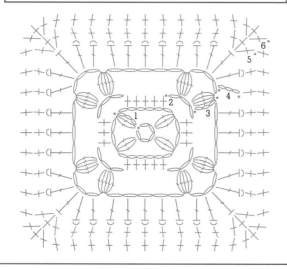

GETTING STARTED

YARN

- Worsted weight yarn in 3 different colors (A, B and C)

The motif shown at left was made using Red Heart Super Saver (100% acrylic, 7oz/198g balls/364yd/333m) in colors 256 carrot (A) and 528 medium purple (B); Red Heart Kids (100% acrylic, 5oz/140g balls/290yd/265m) in color 2650 pistachio (C).

HOOK

- Size K/10½ (6.5mm) crochet hook or any size to obtain gauge

GAUGE

- Rounds 1–2 in pattern = 2½" (6cm)

SPECIAL STITCHES

- beg pop = beginning popcorn
- pop = popcorn (5 dc)
- blp(s) = back loop(s) only

Motif

Note: All rounds are worked on the right side.

With A, ch 5, join with sl st to form ring.

ROUND 1: Beg-cl in ring, ch 2, cl in ring, ch 6, cl in ring, ch 2, cl in ring, ch 6; join with sl st in top of beg-cl—4 cl, 2 ch-2 sps, 2 ch-6 sps. Fasten off.

ROUND 2: Join B with sc in either ch-6 sp, 4 sc in same sp, ch 3, sk 1 cl, 3 sc in ch-2 sp, ch 3, sk 1 cl, 5 sc in ch-6 sp, ch 3, sk 1 cl, 3 sc in ch-2 sp, ch 3, sk 1 cl; join with sl st in first sc—16 sc, 4 ch-3 sps. Fasten off.

ROUND 3: Join C with sl st in either ch-3 beginning a long side, (beg pop, ch 3, pop) in same sp, ch 5, sk 5 sc, (pop, ch 3, pop) in ch-3 sp, ch 3, sk 3 sc, (pop, ch 3, pop) in ch-3 sp, ch 5, sk 5 sc, (pop, ch 3, pop) in ch-3 sp, ch 3, sk 3 sc; join with sl st in top of beg pop—8 pop, 2 ch-5 sps, 6 ch-3 sps. Fasten off.

ROUND 4: Join A with sl st in either ch-3 sp beginning a long side, ch 3 (counts as dc), 4 dc in same sp, sk 1 pop, 5 dc in ch-5 sp, sk pop, 5 dc in ch-3 sp, sk 1 pop, 3 dc in ch-3 sp, sk pop, 5 dc in ch-3 sp, sk 1 pop, 5 dc in ch-5 sp, sk 1 pop, 5 dc in ch-3 sp, sk 1 pop, 3 dc in ch-3 sp; join with sl st in top of beg ch-3—36 dc. Fasten off.

ROUND 5: Join C with sc in middle dc of dc-5 corner beginning either long side, 2 more sc in same st, sc in blp of each of next 9 sts, 3 sc through both loops in next st, sc in blp of each of next 7 sts, 3 sc in next st, sc in blp of each of next 9 sts, 3 sc in next st, sc in blp of each of next 7 sts; join with sl st in first sc—44 sc. Fasten off.

ROUND 6: Join B with sc in both loops of middle sc of 3-sc corner beginning either long side, 2 more sc in same st; *sc in each st to middle sc of next corner, 3 sc in middle sc of sc-3 corner; rep from * 2 more times, sc in each of remaining 9 sts; join with sl st in first sc—52 sc. Fasten off.

Finishing

Weave in all ends.

Mix and Match with these motifs:

Team Captain Motif

Oro Sol Motif

Red Tide Motif

Try-It Triangle Motif

Chair Back Motif

This design is a gift of yarn tied with a bow.

Gift Package
Skill level: Advanced
Finished measurement: 4½" × 5" (11cm × 13cm)

GETTING STARTED

YARN
• Worsted weight yarn in 2 different colors (A and B)

The motif shown at right was made using Red Heart Eco-Ways (70% acrylic, 30% recycled polyester, 4oz/113g balls/186yd/170m) in colors 3114 chamois (A) and 3374 rose dust (B).

HOOK
• Size K/10½ (6.5mm) crochet hook or any size to obtain gauge

GAUGE
• Rounds 1–2 in pattern = 2½" (6cm)

Motif

Note: All rounds are worked on the right side.

With A, ch 4, join with sl st to form ring.

ROUND 1: Ch 1, 8 sc in ring; join with sl st in sc, do not fasten off—8 sc.

ROUND 2: Ch 1, sc in same st; *ch 3, sk 1 st, sc in next st; rep from * 2 more times, ch 3, sk 1 st; join with sl st in first sc—4 sc, 4 ch-3 sps. Fasten off.

ROUND 3: Join B with sl st in any ch-3 sp, ch 3 (counts as dc), 2 dc in same sp, ch 4, 5 dc in next ch-3 sp, ch 4, 3 dc in next ch-3 sp, ch 4, 5 dc in ch-3 sp, ch 4; join with sl st in top of beg ch-3—16 dc, 4 ch-4 sps. Fasten off.

ROUND 4: Join A with sl st in a ch-4 sp starting a short side, ch 3 (counts as dc), 4 dc in same sp; ch 3, sk 3 sts, 5 dc in next ch-4 sp, ch 4, sk 5 sts, 5 dc in next ch-4 sp, ch 3, sk 3 sts, 5 dc in next ch-4 sp, ch 4, sk 5 sts; join with sl st in top of beg ch-3—20 dc, 2 ch-3 sps, 2 ch-4 sps. Fasten off.

ROUND 5: Join B with sl st in middle dc of either 5-dc corner starting a short side, ch 3 (counts as dc), 2 dc in same st, dc in each of next 2 sts, dc in ch-3 sp, FPtr2tog around the first and third dc directly below on round 3, dc in same ch-3 sp, dc in next 2 sts, 3 dc in next st, dc in next 2 sts, FPtr in dc directly below on round 3, 3 dc in ch-3 sp, FPtr in dc directly below on round 3, dc in next 2 sts, 3 dc in next st, dc in each of next 2 sts, dc in ch-3 sp, FPtr2tog around the first and third dc directly below on round 3, dc in same ch-3 sp, dc in next 2 sts, 3 dc in next st, dc in next 2 st, FPtr in dc directly below on round 3, 3 dc in ch-3 sp, FPtr in dc directly below on round 3, dc in last 2 sts; join with sl st in top of beg ch-3—2 FPtr2tog, 4 FPtr, 38 dc. Fasten off.

ROUND 6: Join A with sc in middle dc of a 3-dc corner starting a short side, 2 sc in same st, sc in each of next 4 sts, FPhdc around next st, sc in each of next 4 sts, 3 sc in next st, sc in each of next 3 sts, FPhdc in next st, sc in each of next 3 sts, FPhdc in next st, sc in each of next 3 sts, 3 sc in next st, sc in each of next 4 sts, FPhdc in next st, sc in next 4 sts, 3 sc in next st, sc in each of next 3 sts, FPhdc around next st, sc in next 3 sts, FPhdc around next st, sc in each of last 3 sts; join with sl st in first sc—6 FPhdc, 46 sc. Fasten off.

Finishing

Weave in all ends.

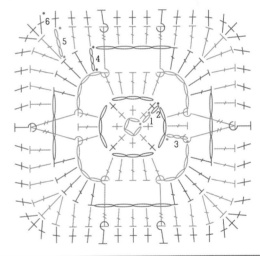

Mix and Match with these motifs:

Cherry Cordial
Motif

Off Center
Motif

Hurricane
Motif

Purple Pansy
Motif

Oscar Square
Motif

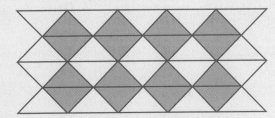
Diamond Layout

TRIANGLES

Dare to be different! I love granny squares but when movement and uniqueness are what you want, you can't go wrong with a triangle.

Triangles are quick and easy, and they add a new dynamic to a blanket. The best thing about triangles is that they lend themselves to optical illusions. When many triangles are put together, it is easy to see poinsettia or flower shapes emerge from the sea of points. Changing colors will create a vastly different appearance in a blanket. How many different combinations can you come up with?

Triangles and hexagons are good friends— they go together like chocolate and peanut butter. When creating your own project, an impressive place to start is by pairing a great triangle with a great hexagon.

Because triangles are often worked in rounds, the points of crocheted triangles tend to be rounded a bit. To combat this, a taller stitch can be placed at the very point in between two shorter stitches. Another way to combat a rounded point is to use a natural fiber and block the motifs into nice, sharp points.

When assembling triangles, the triangles come together and resemble a pie cut into slices. Six triangles will make a hexagon. When six triangles come together to form a hexagon, six points will all join at one vertex. When joining triangles, whether whipstitching or crocheting, make sure they are all secured together at that central vertex so there are no gaps. If it is impossible to close the gap where six triangles come together, a fill-in motif, like a tiny crocheted circle, can be put in the space. Be creative!

There are many ways to achieve different looks with the color placement in triangles. A random color placement leads to a kaleido-scope-type look. Placing the triangles in a row for color sequence can make the project look more graphic or masculine. Placing different colored triangles in a round or starburst pattern can create an almost floral appearance. This is definitely one of those projects where the digital camera can come in handy as you explore all the possibilities.

55

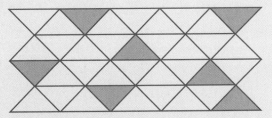
Random Layout

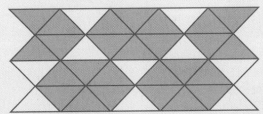
Round Layout

Floating Triangle

Skill level: Beginner | Finished measurement: 4" wide at base × 3¾" tall (10cm × 9.5cm)

Just like this circle can't hover unsupported, no one is an island. Wouldn't this motif make a great triangular prayer shawl?

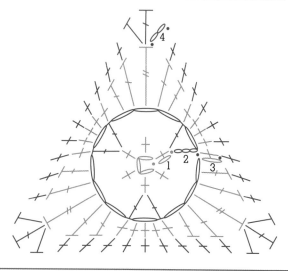

GETTING STARTED

YARN

- Worsted weight yarn in 2 different colors (A and B)

The motif shown at left was made using TLC Essentials (100% acrylic, 6oz/170g balls/312yd/285m) in colors 2680 eden green (A) and 2840 medium lake blue (B).

HOOK

- Size K/10½ (6.5mm) crochet hook or any size to obtain gauge

GAUGE

- Round 1 in pattern = 1" (3cm)

Motif

Note: All rounds are worked on the right side.

With A, ch 3; join with sl st to form ring.

ROUND 1: Ch 1, 6 sc in ring, join with sl st in beg-sc—6 sc. Fasten off.

ROUND 2: Join B with sl st in any st, ch 4 (counts as dc plus ch 1), dc in same st, ch 3, sk next st, *(dc, ch 1, dc) in next st, ch 3, sk next st; rep from * 1 more time; join with sl st in 3rd ch of beg ch-4, do not fasten off—6 dc, 3 ch-1 sps, 3 ch-3 sps.

ROUND 3: Ch 1, sc in same st, 3 sc in next ch-1 sp, sc in next st, (2 dc, tr, 2 dc) in next ch-3 sp; *sc in next st, 3 sc in next ch-1 sp, sc in next st, (2 dc, tr, 2 dc) in ch-3 sp; rep from * 1 more time; join with sl st in first sc—15 sc, 12 dc, 3 tr. Fasten off.

ROUND 4: Join A with sl st in any tr, ch 2 (counts as hdc), (dc, hdc) in same st, sc in each of next 9 sts; *(hdc, dc, hdc) in next st, sc in each of next 9 sts; rep from * 1 more time; join with sl st in top beg ch-2—3 dc, 6 hdc, 27 sc. Fasten off.

Finishing

Weave in all ends.

56

Mix and Match with these motifs:

Simplicity Motif

Octagon Medallion Motif

Golden Hexagon Motif

Cameo Motif

Cherry Cordial Motif

Serene
Skill level: Beginner | Finished measurement: 3½" wide at base × 3¼" tall (9cm × 8cm)

Just looking at it makes me feel centered. Meditate on this triangle for a while and you'll begin to feel serene and calm.

GETTING STARTED

YARN
• Worsted weight yarn in 2 different colors (A and B)

The motif shown at right was made using Red Heart Eco-Ways (70% acrylic, 30% recycled polyester, 4oz/113g balls/186yd/170m) in colors 3520 aquarium (A) and 3360 mushroom (B).

HOOK
• Size I/9 (5.5mm) crochet hook or any size to obtain gauge

GAUGE
• Rounds 1–3 in pattern = 3½" (9cm) sides

Motif

Note: All rounds are worked on the right side.

With A, ch 5; join with sl st to form ring.

ROUND 1: Ch 1, 9 sc in ring; join with sl st in first sc, do not fasten off—9 sc.

ROUND 2: Ch 1, sc in same st; ch 7, sk next 2 sts; *sc in next st, ch 7, sk 2 sts; rep from * 1 more time; join with sl st in first sc—3 sc, 3 ch-7 sps. Fasten off.

ROUND 3: Join B with sc in any ch-7 sp, (sc, 2 hdc, dc, tr, dc, 2 hdc, 2 sc) in same sp, sc in next st; *(2 sc, 2 hdc, dc, tr, dc, 2 hdc, 2 sc) in next ch-7 sp, sc in next st; rep from * 1 more time; join with sl st in first sc—3 tr, 6 dc, 12 hdc, 15 sc. Fasten off.

Finishing

Weave in all ends.

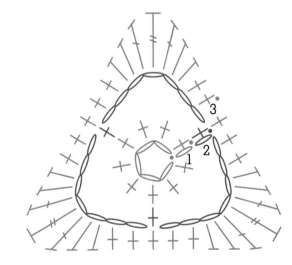

Mix and Match with these motifs:

Floral Octagon Motif

Neapolitan Motif

Brilliant Motif

Star Power Motif

Vintage Motif

57

Recycle

Skill level: Easy | Finished measurement: 4¼" wide at base × 4" tall (11cm × 10cm)

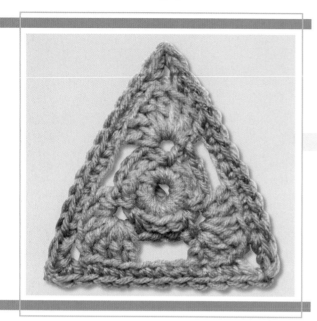

Reminiscent of the green universal symbol for recycle, this design feels fresh and clean.

GETTING STARTED

YARN
- Worsted weight yarn in 2 different colors (A and B)

The motif shown at left was made using Red Heart Kids (100% acrylic, 5oz/141g balls/290yd/265m) in color 2650 pistachio (A); TLC Essentials (100% acrylic, 6oz/170g balls/312yd/285m) in color 2821 paradise blue (B).

HOOK
- Size K/10½ (6.5mm) crochet hook or any size to obtain gauge

GAUGE
- Rounds 1–2 in pattern = 2¼" across (6cm)

SPECIAL STITCHES
- blp(s) = back loop(s) only

Motif

Note: All rounds are worked on the right side.

With color A, ch 5, join with sl st to form ring.

ROUND 1: Ch 1, 12 sc in ring, join with sl st in first sc—12 sc. Fasten off.

ROUND 2: Join B with sc in any sc, (ch 3, sc) in same st; *ch 3, sk 3 sts, (sc, ch 3, sc) in next st; rep from * once, ch 3, sk 3 sts; join with sl st in first sc—6 sc, 6 ch-3 sps. Fasten off.

ROUND 3: Join A with sl st in any ch-3 corner sp, ch 3 (counts as dc), (2 dc, tr, 3 dc) in same sp; *ch 3, sk next ch-3 sp, (3 dc, tr, 3 dc) in next ch-3 sp; rep from * once, ch 3, sk next ch-3 sp; join with sl st in top of beg ch-3—18 dc, 3 tr, 3 ch-3 sps. Fasten off.

ROUND 4: Working blps only; join B with sc in any tr, 2 sc in same st; *sc in next 9 sts, (including chs), 3 sc in next st; rep from * once, sc in next 9 sc; join with sl st in first sc—36 sc. Fasten off.

Finishing

Weave in all ends.

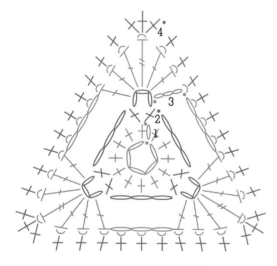

58

Mix and Match with these motifs:

Serene Motif

Eyelets Motif

Bluebonnet Motif

Granny Octagon Motif

Puddles Gather Rain Motif

Whimsy

Skill level: Easy | Finished measurement: 4¼" at base × 4" tall (11cm × 10cm)

It's a pinwheel! Whimsical and fun, this motif reminds me of being at the park in the spring.

GETTING STARTED

YARN
• Worsted weight yarn in 3 different colors (A, B and C)

The motif shown at right was made using Red Heart Kids (100% acrylic, 5oz/141g balls/290yd/265m) in color 2650 pistachio (A); Red Heart Super Saver (100% acrylic, 7oz/198g balls/364yd/333m) in color 579 pale plum (B); TLC Essentials (100% acrylic, 6oz/170g balls/312yd/285m) in color 2500 teal (C).

HOOK
• Size K/10½ (6.5mm) crochet hook or any size to obtain gauge

GAUGE
• Round 1 = 2" across (5cm)

Motif

Note: All rounds are worked on the right side.

With A, ch 5; join with sl st to form ring.

ROUND 1: Beg-cl in ring, ch 5, (cl, ch 5) 2 times in ring; join with sl st in top of beg-cl—3 cl and 3 ch-5 sps. Fasten off.

ROUND 2: Join B with sl st in any ch-5 sp, (beg-cl, ch 3, cl) in same ch-5 sp, ch 5; *(cl, ch 3, cl) in next ch-5 sp, ch 5; rep from * once; join with sl st in top of beg-cl—6 cl, 3 ch-3 sps and 3 ch-5 sps. Fasten off.

ROUND 3: Join C with sc in any ch-3 sp, 4 sc in same sp; *sc in next cl, sc in each of next 5 ch sts, sc in next cl, 5 sc in next ch-3 sp; rep from * once, sc in next cl, sc in each of next 5 ch sts, sc in cl; join with sl st in first sc—36 sc. Fasten off.

Finishing

Weave in all ends.

Mix and Match with these motifs:

Flower Patch Motif

Oro Sol Motif

Purple Pansy Motif

Recycle Motif

Bluebonnet Motif

Beveled

Skill level: Easy | Finished measurement: 4" sides (10cm)

This lightly textured motif reminds me of the bottom of a heavy, ornate wineglass.

GETTING STARTED

YARN

- Worsted weight yarn in 2 different colors (A and B)

The motif shown at left was made using Plymouth Encore Worsted (75% acrylic, 25% wool, 3.5oz/100g balls/200yd/183m) in colors 235 turquoise (A) and 1382 yellow (B).

HOOK

- Size K/10½ (6.5mm) crochet hook or any size to obtain gauge

GAUGE

- Rounds 1–2 in pattern = 2¼" (6cm)

Motif

Note: All rounds are worked on the right side.

With A, ch 4; join with sl st to form ring.

ROUND 1: Beg-cl in ring, ch 3; *cl, ch 3 in ring; rep from * 5 times, ch 3; join with sl st in top of beg-cl—6 cl, 6 ch-3 sp. Fasten off.

ROUND 2: Join B with sl st in any cl, ch 3 (counts as dc), (tr, dc) in same st; *3 dc in ch-3 sp, dc in next st, 3 dc in ch-3 sp, (dc, tr, dc) in next st; rep from * 1 time, 3 dc in ch-3 sp, dc in next st, 3 dc in next ch-3 sp; join with sl st in top of beg ch-3—3 tr, 27 dc. Fasten off.

ROUND 3: Join A with sl st in any tr, ch 2 (counts as hdc), (dc, hdc) in same st; *sc in next 9 sts, (hdc, dc, hdc) in next st; rep from * 1 time, sc in last 9 sts; join with sl st in top of beg ch-2—3 dc, 6 hdc, 27 sc. Fasten off.

Finishing

Weave in all ends.

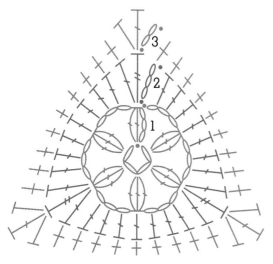

Mix and Match with these motifs:

Drama Queen Motif

Serene Motif

UFO Patch Motif

Oval in a Rectangle Motif

Oscar Square Motif

Campfire

Skill level: Easy | Finished measurement: 4" sides (10cm)

This motif is reminiscent of a crisp morning after a fall campfire.

GETTING STARTED

YARN
- Worsted weight yarn in 3 different colors (A, B and C)

The motif shown at right was made using Caron Simply Soft (100% acrylic, 6oz/170g balls/315yd/288m) in colors 9742 grey heather (A) and 9703 bone (B); Caron Simply Soft Eco (80% acrylic, 20% NatureSpun Post-Consumer Recycled Polyester, 5oz/142g balls/249yd/227m) in color 0033 charcoal (C).

HOOK
- Size K/10½ (6.5mm) crochet hook or any size to obtain gauge

GAUGE
- Rounds 1–2 in pattern = 2¼" (6cm)

SPECIAL STITCHES
- FPhdc = Front Post half double crochet

Motif

Note: All rounds are worked on the right side.

With A, ch 4; join with sl st to form ring.

ROUND 1: (Ch 4, sl st) in ring 6 times—6 ch-4 sp, 6 sl st. Fasten off.

ROUND 2: Join B with sc in any ch-4 sp; *ch 2, (sc, hdc, sc) in next ch-4 sp, ch 2, sc in next ch-4 sp; rep from * 1 time, ch 2, (sc, hdc, sc) in ch-4 sp, ch 2; join with sl st in first sc, do not fasten off—9 sc, 3 hdc.

ROUND 3: Ch 3 (counts as dc); *3 dc in ch-2 sp, dc in next st, (dc, tr, dc) in next st, dc in next st, 3 dc in ch-2 sp, dc in next st; rep from * 1 time, 3 dc in ch-2 sp, dc in next st, (dc, tr, dc) in next st, dc in next st, 3 dc in ch-2 sp; join with sl st in top of beg ch-3—33 dc, 3 tr. Fasten off.

ROUND 4: Join C with sc in 3rd st of any 3-st corner, sc in next 10 sts, FPhdc in next st; *sc in next 11 sc, FPhdc in next st; rep from * 1 time; join with sl st in first sc—3 FPhdc, 33 sc. Fasten off.

Finishing

Weave in all ends.

Mix and Match with these motifs:

Golden Hexagon Motif

Thumbprint Motif

Acapulco Motif

Harvest Motif

Raspberry Tart Motif

Try-It Triangle
Skill level: Easy | Finished measurement: 4" sides (10cm)

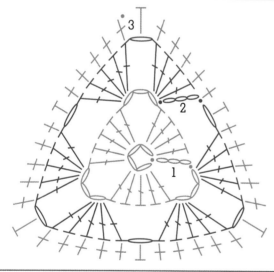

Why not try it? This motif is a nod to America in color, and I made it at the most American of events—a baseball game!

GETTING STARTED

YARN

- Worsted weight yarn in 3 different colors (A, B and C)

The motif shown at left was made using Spud & Chloe, Sweater (55% super-wash wool, 45% organic cotton, 3.5oz/100g hanks/160yd/146m) in colors 7509 firecracker (A), 7506 toast (B) and 7504 lake (C).

HOOK

- Size K/10½ (6.5mm) crochet hook or any size to obtain gauge

GAUGE

- Round 1 in pattern = 2" (5cm) across one side

Motif

Note: All rounds are worked on the right side. Motifs join together easily after being wet blocked to size (see page 13).

With A, ch 4; join with sl st to form ring.

ROUND 1: Ch 3 (counts as dc), 4 dc in ring; *ch 3, 5 dc in ring; rep from * once, ch 3; join with sl st in top of beg ch-3—15 dc, 3 ch-3 sps. Fasten off.

ROUND 2: Join B with sl st in first ch of any ch-3 corner, ch 3 (counts as dc), 4 more dc in same st, ch 1, sk 1 ch, 5 dc in next ch, ch 1, sk 5 sts; *5 dc in next ch, ch 1, sk 1 ch, 5 dc in next ch, ch 1, sk 5 dc; rep from * once; join with sl st in top of beg ch-3—30 dc, 6 ch-1 sps. Fasten off.

ROUND 3: Join C with sc in first st after any ch-1 corner, sc in next 4 dc, hdc in ch-1 sp; *sc in next 5 dc, hdc in ch-1 sp; rep from * 4 more times; join with sl st in first sc—30 sc, 6 hdc. Fasten off.

Finishing

Weave in all ends.

62

Mix and Match with these motifs:

Scary Fun Motif

Granny Octagon Motif

Eyelets Motif

Whimsy Motif

Wrought Iron Motif

Simplicity
Skill level: Easy | Finished measurement: 4" sides (10cm)

This lovely motif is so simple with only three rounds. The fans in the corners and the muted colors give it a Victorian feel.

GETTING STARTED

YARN
• Worsted weight yarn in 2 different colors (A and B)

The motif shown at right was made using Caron Simply Soft (100% acrylic, 6oz/170g balls/315yd/288m) in colors 9719 soft pink (A) and 9722 plum wine (B).

HOOK
• Size K/10½ (6.5mm) crochet hook or any size to obtain gauge

GAUGE
• Rounds 1–2 in pattern = 2¼" (6cm)

SPECIAL STITCHES
• FPhdc = Front Post half double crochet
• FPdc3tog = Front Post double crochet three together

Motif

Note: All rounds are worked on the right side.

With A, ch 3; join with sl st to form ring.

ROUND 1: Ch 3 (counts as dc), 8 dc in ring; join with sl st in top of beg ch-3, do not fasten off—9 dc.

ROUND 2: Ch 3 (counts as dc), dc in same st, 2 dc in each of next 8 sts; join with sl st in top beg-dc—18 dc. Fasten off.

ROUND 3: Join B with sl st in any st, ch 4 (counts as tr), 6 tr in same st; *ch 2, sk 1 st, FPdc3tog in next 3 sts, ch 2, sk 1 st, 7 tr in next st; rep from * 1 time, ch 2, FPdc3tog in next 3 sts, ch 2, sk 1 st; join with sl st in top of beg ch 4—21 tr, 3 FPdc3tog, 6 ch-2 sps. Fasten off.

Finishing

Weave in all ends.

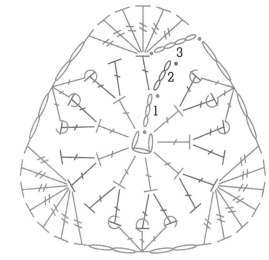

Mix and Match with these motifs:

Floating Triangle Motif

Rose Octagon Motif

Red Tide Motif

Polka Dot Motif

Chair Back Motif

Off Center

Skill level: Intermediate | Finished measurement: 4" wide at base × 3¾" tall (10cm × 9.5cm)

Why be symmetrical? Much of the beauty in nature is asymmetrical, so we should have fun being a little off center! Combine these in a variety of colors for a great blanket for someone who keeps you feeling spontaneous.

GETTING STARTED

YARN
• Worsted weight yarn in 3 different colors (A, B and C)

The motif shown at left was made using Caron Simply Soft (100% acrylic, 6oz/170g balls/315yd/288m) in colors 9703 bone (A), 9707 dark sage (B) and 9726 soft yellow (C).

HOOK
• Size K/10½ (6.5mm) crochet hook or any size to obtain gauge

GAUGE
• Rounds 1–2 in pattern = 2¼" across (6cm)

Motif

Note: All rounds are worked on the right side.

With A, ch 4; join with sl st to form ring.

ROUND 1: Ch 4 (counts as tr), 6 tr in ring, ch 4, cl in ring, ch 4; join with sl st in top beg ch-4—7 tr, 1 cl, 2 ch-4 sps. Fasten off.

ROUND 2: Join B with sc in cl, 6 sc in next ch-4 sp, 2 sc in each of next 7 sts, 6 sc in next ch-4 sp; join with sl st in first sc—27 sc. Fasten off.

ROUND 3: Join C with sc in st above cl; *sc in next st, hdc in each of next 2 sts, dc in each of next 2 sts, tr in each of next 2 sts, ch 2, sk 1 st**, sc in next st; rep from * once; rep from * to ** once; join with sl st in first sc, do not fasten off—6 sc, 6 hdc, 6 dc, 6 tr, 3 ch-2 sps.

ROUND 4: Ch 1, sc in same st, sc in each of next 6 sts; *3 sc in next st, 2 sc in next ch-2 sp**, sc in each of next 7 sts; rep from * once; rep from * to ** once; join with sl st in first sc—36 sc. Fasten off.

Finishing

Weave in all ends.

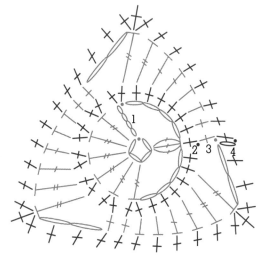

Mix and Match with these motifs:

Pick a Posie Motif

South Beach Motif

Twinkle Motif

Try-It Triangle Motif

Purple Sunset Motif

Acapulco
Skill level: Intermediate | Finished measurement: 4½" wide at base × 4¼" tall (11.5cm × 11cm)

Can you hear the Calypso music playing in the background? Inspired by the blue sky, the warm sun and a fruity drink, this motif says "Acapulco." An interesting mix of post stitches and long stitches makes this triangle a textural little gem.

GETTING STARTED

YARN
• Worsted weight yarn in 3 different colors (A, B and C)

The motif shown at right was made using TLC Essentials (100% acrylic, 6oz/170g balls/312yd/285m) in colors 2820 robin egg (A) and 2690 fusion (B); Red Heart Super Saver (100% acrylic, 7oz/198g balls/364yd/333m) in color 321 gold (C).

HOOK
• Size K/10½ (6.5mm) crochet hook or any size to obtain gauge

GAUGE
• Rounds 1–2 in pattern = 2¼" across (6cm)

Motif

Note: All rounds are worked on the right side.

With color A, ch 4, join with sl st to form ring.

ROUND 1: Ch 3 (counts as dc), 2 dc in ring, ch 4; (3 dc, ch 4) 2 times in ring; join with sl st in top of beg ch-3—9 dc, 3 ch-4 sps. Fasten off.

ROUND 2: Join B with sc in any ch-4 sp; *FPdc around each of next 3 dc, (sc, ch 4, sc) in next ch-4 sp; rep from * once, FPdc around next 3 dc, sc in ch-4 sp, ch 4; join with sl st in first sc—9 FPdc, 6 sc, 3 ch-4 sps. Fasten off.

ROUND 3: Join C with sc in any ch-4 sp; *(sc, long dc in ch-4 sp of round 1, 2 sc) in same ch-4 sp of current round, sc in next st, [working behind the FPdc of round 2, dc in next dc on round 1, sc in next st in round 2] 2 times**, sc in next ch-4 sp; rep from * once; rep from * to ** once; join with sl st in first sc—9 dc, 21 sc. Fasten off.

ROUND 4: Join A with sc in any dc of any corner, (hdc, sc) in same st; *sc in next 9 sts, (sc, hdc, sc) in next st; rep from * 2 times, sc in next 9 sts; join with sl st in first sc—3 hdc, 33 sc. Fasten off.

Finishing

Weave in all ends.

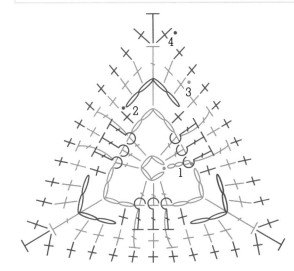

Mix and Match with these motifs:

Simplicity Motif

Hurricane Motif

South Beach Motif

Team Captain Motif

Whimsy Motif

Hexagons

Hexagons are the new black. They are often more interesting than squares, but still make a great fabric with no gaps when tiled together. Keep your eyes open for hexagons in your world. It's very common to see hexagon tile floors, carpet and brick patterns. Let them inspire you to make your own hexagon creation.

Six-sided hexagons fit together perfectly without gaps when putting sides together. The edges of the finished project will be irregular unless the gaps around the edges are filled in with half-hexagons or two or three triangles.

The easiest way to assemble hexagons is by arranging them in columns, and then carefully letting the columns jog together to form an offset pattern.

In addition to fitting together with other hexagons, hexagons fit naturally with triangles since a hexagon is made of of six triangles.

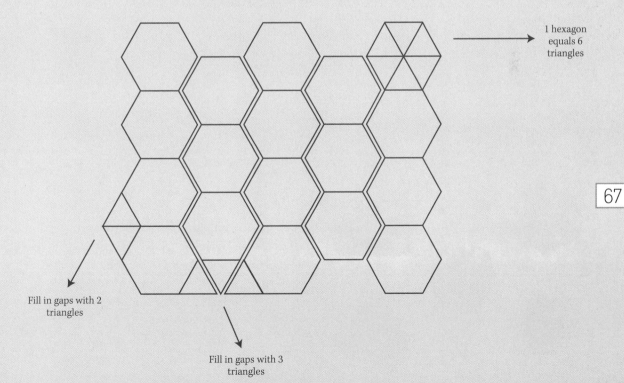

1 hexagon equals 6 triangles

Fill in gaps with 2 triangles

Fill in gaps with 3 triangles

Golden Hexagon

Skill level: Easy | Finished measurement: 5" (13cm) side to side

Who wouldn't love this little pansy? It reminds me of daffodils. I love the fluted, long treble crochet stitches. Crochet up a bouquet of these blooms!

GETTING STARTED

YARN

- Worsted weight yarn in 3 different colors (A, B and C)

The motif shown at left was made using Caron Simply Soft (100% acrylic, 6oz/170g balls/315yd/288m) in colors 9703 bone (A), 9722 plum wine (B) and 9945 sunshine (C).

HOOK

- Size K/10½ (6.5mm) crochet hook or any size to obtain gauge

GAUGE

- Rounds 1–2 in pattern = 3" (8cm)

Motif

Note: All rounds are worked on the right side.

With color A, ch 4; join with sl st to form ring.

ROUND 1: Beg-cl in ring, ch 2, (cl, ch 2) in ring 5 times; join with sl st in top of beg-cl—6 cl and 6 ch-2 sps. Fasten off.

ROUND 2: Join color B with sl st in any ch-2 sp, (beg-cl, ch 2, cl) in same sp, ch 1, (cl, ch 2, cl, ch 1) in each ch-2 sp to end; join with sl st in top of beg-cl—12 cl, 6 ch-2 corner sps and 6 ch-1 side sps. Fasten off.

ROUND 3: Join color C with sl st in any ch-2 sp, ch 4 (counts as tr), (2 tr, ch 3, 3 tr) in same sp, ch 1; *sk next ch-1 sp, (3 tr, ch 3, 3 tr, ch 1) in next ch-2 sp; rep from * to end, sk next ch-1 sp; join with sl st in top of beg ch-4, do not fasten off—36 tr, 6 ch-3 sps and 6 ch-1 sps.

ROUND 4: Ch 1, sc in same st, sc in next 2 sts; *5 sc in next ch-3 sp, sc in next 3 sts, sc in next ch-1 sp**, sc in next 3 sts; rep from * around, ending last rep at **; join with sl st in first sc—72 sc. Fasten off.

Finishing

Weave in all ends.

Mix and Match with these motifs:

Bluebonnet Motif

Neapolitan Motif

Rose Octagon Motif

Pick a Posie Motif

Floating Triangle Motif

Flowery Day

Skill level: Easy | Finished measurement: 5" (13cm) point to point

Here is a bloom that the deer can't eat! Enjoy these blossoms all year long. The peach flowers pop from the foliage green background.

GETTING STARTED

YARN

• Worsted weight yarn in 2 different colors (A and B)

The motif shown at right was made using Red Heart Eco-Ways (70% acrylic, 30% recycled polyester, 4oz/113g balls/186yd/170m) in colors 3422 yam (A) and 1615 lichen (B).

HOOK

• Size K/10½ (6.5mm) crochet hook or any size to obtain gauge

GAUGE

• Rounds 1–3 in pattern = 3½" (9cm)

Motif

Note: All rounds are worked on the right side.

With color A, ch 4, join with sl st to form ring.

ROUND 1: Ch 3, (counts as first dc) 11 dc in ring; join with sl st in top of beg ch-3, do not fasten off—12 dc.

ROUND 2: Ch 1, sc in same st, ch 6, sk 1 st; *sc in next st, ch 6, sk 1 st; rep from * 5 more times; join with sl st in first sc, do not fasten off—6 sc, 6 ch-6 sps.

ROUND 3: Ch 1, sc in first st, 7 sc in ch-6 sp; *sc in next st, 7 sc in ch-6 sp; rep from * 4 more times; join with sl st in first sc—48 sc. Fasten off.

ROUND 4: Join B with sc in 2nd sc of any 7-sc group, sc in next st, 3 sc in next st, sc in next 2 sts, ch 3, sk 3 sts; *sc in next 2 sts, 3 sc in next st, sc in next 2 sts, ch 3, sk 3 sts; rep from * 4 more times; join with sl st in first sc, do not fasten off—6 ch-3 sps, 42 sc.

ROUND 5: Ch 1, sc in first st, sc in next 2 sts, 3 sc in next st; *sc in next 3 sts, ch 3, sk ch-3 sp, sc in next 3 sts**, 3 sc in next st; rep from * 4 more times; rep from * to ** once; join with sl st in first sc—6 ch-3 sps, 54 sc. Fasten off.

Finishing

Weave in all ends.

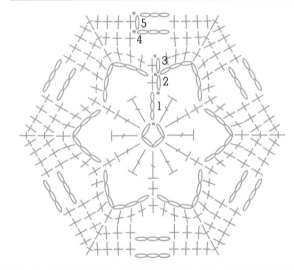

Mix and Match with these motifs:

Last Blueberry Motif

Floral Octagon Motif

Whimsy Motif

Flower Patch Motif

Bluebonnet Motif

Harvest

Skill level: Easy | Finished measurement: 6¼" (16cm) point to point

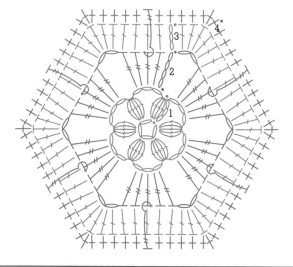

Hardy mums in the fall are very common in our part of middle America. I love the dimension on this one, easily created with popcorn stitches.

GETTING STARTED

YARN

- Worsted weight yarn in 2 different colors (A and B)

The motif shown at left was made using Universal Yarns Deluxe Worsted (100% wool, 3.5oz/100g balls/220yd/200m) in colors 12182 gold spice (A) and 12183 city turf (B).

HOOK

- Size K/10½ (6.5mm) crochet hook or any size to obtain gauge

GAUGE

- Rounds 1–2 in pattern = 3½" (9cm) side to side

SPECIAL STITCHES

- beg pop = beginning popcorn
- pop = popcorn (5 dc)

Motif

Note: All rounds are worked on the right side.

With A, ch 4; join with sl st to form ring.

ROUND 1: Beg pop in ring; *ch 3, pop in ring; rep from * 4 more times; ch 3; join with sl st in top of beg pop—6 pop, 6 ch-3 sps. Fasten off.

ROUND 2: Join B with sl st in any ch-3 sp, ch 4 (counts as tr), 4 more tr in same sp, ch 2; *5 tr in next st, ch 2; rep from * 4 more times; join with sl st in top beg ch-4, do not fasten off—30 tr, 6 ch-2 sps.

ROUND 3: Ch 3 (counts as dc), dc in each of next 4 sts, 5 dc in next ch-2 sp; *dc in each of next 5 sts, 5 dc in ch-2 sp; rep from * 4 more times; join with sl st in top of beg ch-3—60 dc. Fasten off.

ROUND 4: Join A with sc in middle dc of a 5-dc corner, 2 sc in same st, sc in each of next 4 sts; *FPtr around middle tr of 5-tr group in round 2, sk the st behind the FPtr just made, sc in each of the next 4 sts**, 3 sc in next st, sc in each of next 4 sts; rep from * 4 more times; rep from * to ** once—6 FPtr, 66 sc. Fasten off.

Finishing

Weave in all ends.

Mix and Match with these motifs:

Eyelets Motif

Purple Sunset Motif

Polka Dot Motif

Acapulco Motif

Twinkle Motif

Hurricane
Skill level: Intermediate | Finished measurement: 6" (15cm) side to side

For my friend who had a thriving nursery before Hurricane Katrina; the pink is the eye of the storm, the yellow is the hope of the future.

GETTING STARTED

YARN
• Worsted weight yarn in 4 different colors (A, B, C and D)

The motif shown at right was made using Caron Simply Soft Brites (100% acrylic, 6oz/170g balls/315yd/288m) in colors 9604 watermelon (A), 9607 limelight (B) and 9608 blue mint (C); Caron Simply Soft Eco (80% acrylic, 20% NatureSpun Post-Consumer Recycled Polyester, 6 oz/170g balls/315yd/288m) in color 0014 sundrop (D).

HOOK
• Size K/10½ (6.5mm) crochet hook or any size to obtain gauge

GAUGE
• Rounds 1–3 in pattern = 3" (8cm)

SPECIAL STITCHES
• Picot: ch 3, sl st in 2nd ch from hook

Motif

Note: All rounds are worked on the right side.

With A, ch 3, join with sl st to form ring.

ROUND 1: Ch 6 (counts as tr plus 2 ch), (tr, ch 2) in ring 5 times; join with sl st in top of beg ch-4—6 tr, 6 ch-2 sps. Fasten off.

ROUND 2: Join B with sc in any tr, sc in same st; *2 sc in next ch-2 sp, 2 sc in next tr; rep from * 4 times, 2 sc in next ch-2 sp; join with sl st in first sc—24 sc. Fasten off.

ROUND 3: Join C with sc in any sc; *picot, ch 2, sk 3 sts**, sc in next st; rep from * 4 more times; rep from * to ** once; join with sl st in first sc—6 sc, 6 picots. Fasten off.

ROUND 4: Join D with sc in any picot; *ch 6, sk next sc, sc in next picot, rep from * 5 times, ch 6; join with sl st in first sc, do not fasten off—6 sc, 6 ch-6 sps.

ROUND 5: Ch 1, sc in same st; *3 sc in next ch-6 sp, long dc into sc 1 row below, 3 sc in same ch-6 sp**, 1 sc in next st; rep from * 4 more times; rep from * to ** once; join with sl st in first sc, do not fasten off—42 sc, 6 dc.

ROUND 6: Ch 1, 3 sc in first st, sc in next 7 sts; *3 sc in next st, sc in each of next 7 sts; rep from * 4 more times; join with sl st in first sc, do not fasten off—60 sc.

ROUND 7: Ch 3 (counts as dc); *3 dc in next st, dc in next 9 sts; rep from * 4 more times, 3 dc in next st, dc in last 8 sts; join with sl st in top beg ch-3—72 dc. Fasten off.

Finishing

Weave in all ends.

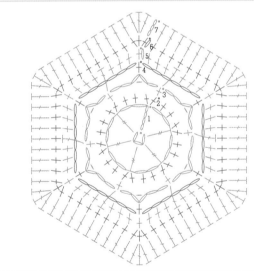

Mix and Match with these motifs:

Gift Package Motif

Oro Sol Motif

Stain Berry Motif

Golden Hexagon Motif

Try-It Triangle Motif

Bluebonnet

Skill level: Intermediate | Finished measurement: 6" (15cm) side to side

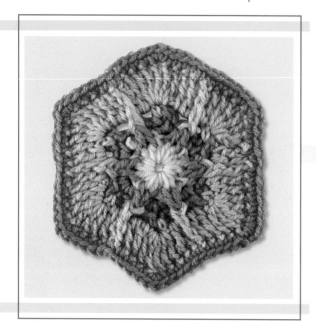

This design reminds me of bluebonnet flowers. Pretty and cheerful, these unassuming flowers are just sweet.

GETTING STARTED

YARN

• Worsted weight yarn in 3 different colors (A, B and C)

The motif shown at left was made using TLC Essentials (100% acrylic, 6oz/170g balls/312yd/285m) in colors 2220 butter (A) and 2830 lake blue (C); Red Heart Super Saver (100% acrylic, 7oz/198g balls/364yd/333m) in color 0885 delft blue (B).

HOOK

• Size K/10½ (6.5mm) crochet hook or any size to obtain gauge

GAUGE

• Rounds 1–2 in pattern = 3" (8cm)

Motif

Note: All rounds are worked on the right side.

With A, ch 4, join with sl st to form ring.

ROUND 1: Beg-cl in ring, (ch 2, cl) 5 times in ring, ch 2; join with sl st in top of beg cl—6 cl, 6 ch-2 sp. Fasten off.

ROUND 2: Join B with sc in any cl, ch 3, sc in same st; *in ch-2 sp: (sc, dc2tog around the last leg of the first cl, and the first leg of the next cl, sc in same ch-2 sp), in cl: (sc, ch 3, sc); rep from * 4 more times, sc in ch-2 sp, dc2tog, sc in same ch-2 sp; join with sl st in first sc—6 dc2tog, 24 sc, 6 ch-3 sps. Fasten off.

ROUND 3: Join C with sc in any ch-3 sp; *ch 5, sk 5 sts, sc in next ch-3 sp; rep from * 4 more times, ch 5; join with sl st in first sc, do not fasten off—6 sc, 6 ch-5 sps.

ROUND 4: Ch 4 (counts as tr), 4 tr in same st; *2 tr in ch-5 sp, FPtr around both legs of the dc2tog that is 2 rows below on round 2, 2 tr in same ch-5 sp, 5 tr in next sc; rep from * 4 more times, 2 tr in ch-5 sp, FPtr around next st, 2 tr in ch-5 sp; join with sl st in top of beg ch-4—54 tr, 6 FPtr. Fasten off.

ROUND 5: Join B with sc in 3rd tr of tr-5 corner, 2 sc in same st; *sc in next 9 sts, 3 sc in next st; rep from * 4 more times, sc in last 9 sts; join with sl st in first sc—72 sc. Fasten off.

Finishing

Weave in all ends.

72

Mix and Match with these motifs:

Purple Sunset Motif

Harvest Motif

Acapulco Motif

Oscar Square Motif

Vintage Motif

Red Tide

Skill level: Intermediate | Finished measurement: 6" (15cm) point to point

The rippling texture reminds me of a wave in the ocean during the enigmatic red tide. Certainly there must be red tropical fish, too?

GETTING STARTED

YARN
• Worsted weight yarn in 3 different colors (A, B and C)

The motif shown at right was made using Bernat Satin (100% acrylic, 3.5oz/100g balls/163yd/149m) in colors 04531 rouge (A), 04222 fern (B) and 04141 sapphire (C).

HOOK
• Size K/10½ (6.5mm) crochet hook or any size to obtain gauge

GAUGE
• Rounds 1–2 in pattern = 3" (8cm)

SPECIAL STITCHES
• beg pop = beginning popcorn
• pop = popcorn (5 dc)

Motif

Note: All rounds are worked on the right side.

With A, ch 3; join with sl st to form ring.

ROUND 1: Ch 4 (counts as dc plus 1 ch), (dc, ch 1) 5 times in ring; join with sl st in 3rd ch of beg ch-4, do not fasten off—6 dc, 6 ch-1 sps.

ROUND 2: Beg pop in first st, ch 4, sk ch-1 sp; *pop in next st, ch 4, sk ch-1 sp; rep from * 4 more times; join with sl st in top of beg pop—6 pop, 6 ch-4 sps. Fasten off.

ROUND 3: Join B with sl st in any ch-4 sp, ch 4 (counts as first tr), 6 more tr in same sp; *ch 2, sk pop, 7 tr in next ch-4 sp; rep from * 4 more times, ch 2, sk pop; join with sl st in top of beg ch-4—42 tr, 6 ch-2 sps. Fasten off.

ROUND 4: Join C with sl st in any ch-2 sp, ch 3 (counts as dc), 2 dc in same sp, BPdc around next 7 sts; *3 dc in ch-2 sp, BPdc around next 7 sts; rep from * 4 more times; join with sl st in top of beg ch-3—42 BPdc, 18 dc. Fasten off.

ROUND 5: Join A with sc in middle dc of any 3-dc corner group, 2 sc in same st, sc in each of next 9 sts; *3 sc in next st, sc in each of next 9 sts; rep from * 4 more times; join with sl st in first sc—72 sc. Fasten off.

Finishing

Weave in all ends.

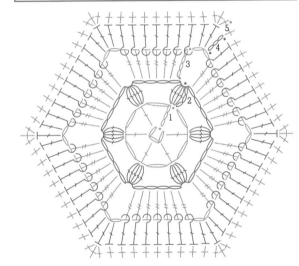

Mix and Match with these motifs:

Polka Dot Motif

Team Captain Motif

Pick a Posie Motif

UFO Patch Motif

Drama Queen Motif

Twinkle

Skill level: Intermediate | Finished measurement: 6½" (17cm) point to point

The "Twinkle, Twinkle, Little Star" lyrics were written by sisters Ann and Jane Taylor to a snippet of Mozart's "Variations for Piano." This little motif reminds me of that quintessential childhood tune.

GETTING STARTED

YARN

- Worsted weight yarn in 2 different colors (A and B)

The motif shown at left was made using Bernat Satin (100% acrylic, 3.5oz/100g balls/163yd/149m) in colors 04141 sapphire (A) and 04221 soft fern (B).

HOOK

- Size K/10½ (6.5mm) crochet hook or any size to obtain gauge

GAUGE

- Rounds 1–3 in pattern = 4" (10cm)

Motif

Note: All rounds are worked on the right side.

With A, ch 4; join with sl st to form ring.

ROUND 1: Ch 3 (counts as first dc), 11 dc in ring; join with sl st in top beg ch-3, do not fasten off—12 dc.

ROUND 2: Ch 1, sc in first st, ch 7, sk 1 st; *sc in next st, ch 7, sk 1 st; rep from * 4 more times; join with sl st in first sc—6 sc, 6 ch-7 sps. Fasten off.

ROUND 3: Join B with sc in any sc, sc in next 7 ch sts; *sc in next sc, sc in next 7 ch sts; rep from * 4 more times; join with sl st in first sc—48 sc. Fasten off.

ROUND 4: Join A with sc in 4th sc of 7-sc side; *ch 3, sk 3 sc, dc in next st, ch 3**; sk 3 sts, sc in next sc; rep from * 4 more times, rep from * to ** once; join with sl st in first sc, do not fasten off—6 dc, 6 sc, 12 ch-3 sps.

ROUND 5: Ch 3 (counts as first dc), 2 dc in same st, 3 dc in next ch-3 sp, dc in next st, 3 dc in ch-3 sp; *3 dc in next st, 3 dc in ch-3 sp, dc in next st, 3 dc in ch-3 sp; rep from * 4 more times; join with sl st in top of beg ch-3—60 dc. Fasten off.

ROUND 6: Join B with sc in middle dc of any 3-dc corner, 2 sc in same st, sc in next 9 sts; *3 sc in next sc, sc in next 9 sts; rep from * 4 more times; join with sl st in first sc—72 sc. Fasten off.

Finishing

Weave in all ends.

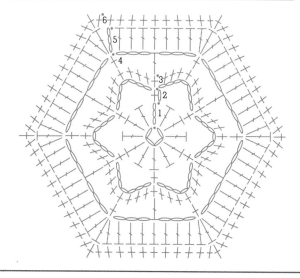

Mix and Match with these motifs:

Cherry Cordial Motif

Beveled Motif

Red Tide Motif

Purple Pansy Motif

Floating Triangle Motif

74

Wrought Iron
Skill level: Intermediate | Finished measurement: 4½" (11cm) side to side

As a child, I would trace with my finger the intricate twists and turns of the wrought-iron rail that lined the sides of our porch. In this motif, the spaces are just as interesting as the stitches.

GETTING STARTED

YARN

• Worsted weight yarn in 2 different colors (A and B)

The motif shown at right was made using Universal Yarns Deluxe Worsted (100% wool, 3.5oz/100g balls/220yd/201m) in colors 12204 pussywillow gray (A) and 12172 dark crystal (B).

HOOK

• Size K/10½ (6.5mm) crochet hook or any size to obtain gauge

GAUGE

• Rounds 1–2 in pattern = 3" (8cm)

Motif

Note: All rounds are worked on the right side.

With A, ch 4; join with sl st to form ring.

ROUND 1: Ch 7 (counts as tr plus ch 3); *(tr, ch 3) in ring 5 more times; join with sl st in 4th ch of beg ch-7, do not fasten off—6 tr, 6 ch-3 sps.

ROUND 2: Beg cl, ch 5, sk next ch-3 sp; *cl in next tr, ch 5, sk next ch-3 sp; rep from * 5 more times; join with sl st in top first cl—6 cl, 6 ch-5 sps. Fasten off.

ROUND 3: Join B with sc in any cl, ch 5, sc in same st; *5 sc in ch-5 sp, (sc, ch 5, sc) in next cl; rep from * 4 more times; 5 sc in next ch-5 sp, join with sl st in first sc, do not fasten off—6 ch-5 sps, 42 sc.

ROUND 4: *7 sc in next ch-5 sp, ch 5, sk next 7 sc; rep from * 5 more times; join with sl st in first sc—6 ch-5 sps, 42 sc. Fasten off.

Finishing

Weave in all ends.

Mix and Match with these motifs:

Vintage Motif

Eyelets Motif

Cameo Motif

Granny Octagon Motif

Beveled Motif

Brilliant

Skill level: Intermediate | Finished measurement: 6½" (17cm) point to point

Like the brilliant cut of a diamond, this hexagon's intricacy commands attention.

GETTING STARTED

YARN

• Worsted weight yarn in 2 different colors (A and B)

The motif shown at left was made using Louet Gems Chunky (100% merino wool, 3.5oz/100g hanks/94yd/86m) in colors 66 bright blue (A) and 42 eggplant (B).

HOOK

• Size K/10½ (6.5mm) crochet hook or any size to obtain gauge

GAUGE

• Rounds 1–2 in pattern = 3" (8cm)

Motif

Note: All rounds are worked on the right side.

With A, ch 5; join with sl st to form ring.

ROUND 1: Ch 1, 12 sc in ring; join with sl st in first sc, do not fasten off—12 sc.

ROUND 2: Ch 6 (counts as tr plus 2 ch); *tr in next st, ch 2; rep from * 10 more times; join with sl st in 4th ch of beg ch-6—12 tr, 12 ch-2 sps. Fasten off.

ROUND 3: Join B with sl st in any ch-2 sp, ch 5 (counts as dc plus 2 ch), dc in same sp; *FPdc around next tr, (dc, ch 2, dc) in next ch-2 sp; rep from * 10 more times; FPdc around next tr; join with sl st in 3rd ch of beg ch-5—12 FPdc, 24 dc. Fasten off.

ROUND 4: Join A with sc in any ch-2 sp, 2 more sc in same sp; *sk 1 st, FPdc around next st, sk 1 st, (sc, ch 2, sc) in next ch-2 sp, sk 1 st, FPdc around next st**, sk 1 st, 3 sc in next ch-2 sp; rep from * 4 more times; rep from * to ** once; join with sl st in first sc—60 sc, 12 FPdc and 6 ch-2 sps. Fasten off.

ROUND 5: Join B with sl st in the middle sc of any 3-sc group, ch 4 (counts as a hdc plus ch 2); *sk next 3 sts, (cl, ch 3, cl) in ch-2 sp, ch 2, sk 3 sts**, hdc in next sc of ch 2; rep from * 4 more times; rep from * to ** once; join with sl st in 2nd ch of beg ch-4, do not fasten off—12 cl, 6 hdc.

ROUND 6: Ch 1, sc in same st; *2 sc in ch-2 sp, sc in cl, 5 sc in ch-3 sp, sc in next st, 2 sc in ch-2 sp**, sc in next st; rep from * 4 more times; rep from * to ** once; join with sl st in first sc—72 sc. Fasten off.

Finishing

Weave in all ends.

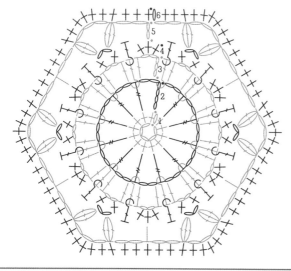

Mix and Match with these motifs:

Golden Hexagon Motif

Scary Fun Motif

Cherry Cordial Motif

Off Center Motif

Hurricane Motif

UFO Patch

Skill level: Advanced | Finished measurement: 6½" (17cm) point to point

This could be a modern patch on an astronaut's uniform. Cue commanding music!

GETTING STARTED

YARN

• Worsted weight yarn in 2 different colors (A and B)

The motif shown at right was made using Bernat Satin (100% acrylic, 3.5oz/100g balls/163yd/149m) in colors 04203 teal (A) and 04221 soft fern (B).

HOOK

• Size K/10½ (6.5mm) crochet hook or any size to obtain gauge

GAUGE

• Rounds 1–3 in pattern 3½" (9cm) across one side

Motif

Note: All rounds are worked on the right side.

With A, ch 4, join with sl st to form ring.

ROUND 1: Ch 3 (counts as dc), 4 dc in ring; *ch 2, 5 dc in ring, rep from * once, ch 2; join with sl st in top of beg ch-3—15 dc, 3 ch-2 sps. Fasten off.

ROUND 2: Join B with sl st in 5th dc of a 5-dc group before any ch-2 corner sp, ch 3 (counts as dc), 4 dc in same st, ch 3, sk ch-2 sp, 5 dc in next st, ch 1, sk 3 sts, 5 dc in next st, ch 3, sk ch-2 sp, 5 dc in next st, ch 1, sk 3 sts, 5 dc in next st, ch 3, sk ch-2 sp, 5 dc in next st, ch 1; join with sl st in top of beg ch-3—30 dc, 3 ch-3 sps, 3 ch-1 sps. Fasten off.

ROUND 3: Working behind round 2, join A with sl st in any ch-2 sp in round 1, ch 4 (counts as tr), 4 tr in same sp, ch 3, sk 5 sts on round 2, 5 tr in middle dc of next 5-dc group in round 1, ch 3; *5 tr in next ch-2 sp in round 1, ch 3, 5 tr in middle dc of dc-5 group on round 1, ch 3; rep from * 1 more time; join with sl st in top of beg ch-4, do not fasten off—30 tr, 6 ch-3 sps.

ROUND 4: Ch 3 (counts as dc), dc in next 4 sts; *(2 dc, tr, 2 dc) in ch-3 corner sp, dc in next 5 sts; rep from * 4 more times; (2 dc, tr, 2 dc) in ch-3 sp; join with sl st in top of beg ch-3—6 tr, 54 dc. Fasten off.

ROUND 5: Join B with sc in a corner tr prior to any ch-3 corner sp in round 2, 2 sc in same st; *sc in next 4 sts, working in front of round 3, long dc in next unused ch-3 sp in round 2, sk 1 st on round 5 behind dc just worked, sc in next 4 sts, 3 sc in next st, sc in each of next 9 sts**, 3 sc in next st; rep from * once; rep from * to ** once; join with sl st in first sc—3 dc, 69 sc. Fasten off.

Finishing

Weave in all ends.

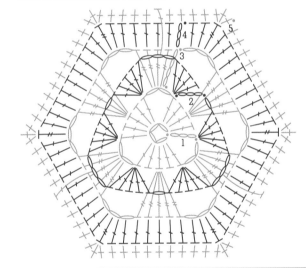

Mix and Match with these motifs:

Wrought Iron Motif

Stain Berry Motif

Oro Sol Motif

Recycle Motif

Thumbprint Motif

OCTAGONS

Think of an octagon as a big square with the corners cut off. When four of these shapes are placed next to one another, a square-shaped empty space will be created in the center. You can either fill this space with a square motif or leave it open as a design element. (Keep in mind that the space is likely to be big enough for a fist to go through.) For this reason, octagons and squares are usually paired together. Since some triangles are half-squares, triangles can also help fill in the spaces left by octagons. You can also use half-square triangles to to fill in border gaps or in pairs in place of squares.

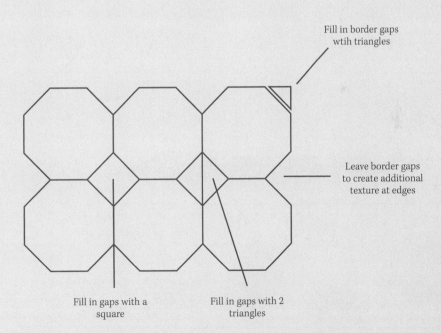

Fill in border gaps wtih triangles

Leave border gaps to create additional texture at edges

Fill in gaps with a square

Fill in gaps with 2 triangles

Rose Octagon
Skill level: Beginner | Finished measurement: 6" (15cm) point to point

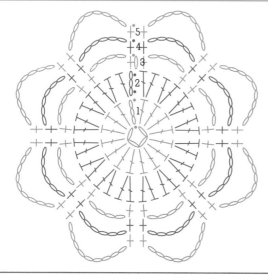

No other yarn can capture the velvety depth of the rose like these shades of red. Does it make you want to bury your nose in it? Or maybe call to mind rose water perfume?

GETTING STARTED

YARN
- Worsted weight yarn in 4 different colors (A, B, C and D)

The motif shown at left was made using Blue Sky Alpacas Worsted Hand Dyes (50% royal alpaca, 50% merino wool, 3.5oz/100g hanks/100yd/91m) in colors 2012 cranberry (A), 2000 red (B), 2026 petunia (C) and 2018 strawberry (D).

HOOK
- Size K/10½ (6.5mm) crochet hook or any size to obtain gauge

GAUGE
- Rounds 1–2 in pattern = 3" (8cm)

Motif

Note: All rounds are worked on the right side.

With color A, ch 4; join with sl st to form ring.

ROUND 1: Ch 3 (counts as dc), 15 dc in ring; join with sl st in top of beg ch-3—16 dc. Fasten off.

ROUND 2: Join B with sl st in any st, ch 3 (counts as dc), dc in same st, 2 dc in each of next 15 sts; join with sl st in top of beg ch-3, do not fasten off—32 dc.

ROUND 3: Ch 1, sc in same st; *ch 4, sk next 2 sts, sc in each of next 2 sts; rep from * 6 more times, ch 4, sk next 2 sts, sc in last st; join with sl st in beg sc—16 sc and 8 ch-4 sps. Fasten off.

ROUND 4: Join C with sc where previously fastened off; *ch 6, sk next ch-4 sp, sc in each of next 2 sts; rep from * 6 more times, ch 6, sk next ch-4 sp, sc in last st; join with sl st in first sc—16 sc and 8 ch-6 sps. Fasten off.

ROUND 5: Join D with sc where previously fastened off; *ch 9, sk next ch-6 sp, sc in each of next 2 sts; rep from * 6 more times, ch 9, sk next ch-6 sp, sc in last st; join with sl st in beg-sc—16 sc and 8 ch-9 sps. Fasten off.

Finishing

Weave in all ends.

Mix and Match with these motifs:

UFO Patch Motif

Purple Pansy Motif

Try-It Triangle Motif

Team Captain Motif

Neapolitan Motif

Oro Sol

Skill level: Beginner | Finished measurement: 6¾" (17cm) point to point

This motif is named Oro Sol, which is Spanish for "golden sun." It's how I imagine vibrant sunshine might look over the Mayan ruins of Mexico.

GETTING STARTED

YARN
- Worsted weight yarn in 3 different colors (A, B and C)

The motif shown at right was made using Universal Yarns Deluxe Worsted (100% wool, 3.5oz/100g balls/220yd/200m) in colors 12204 pussywillow gray (A), 41795 nectarine (B) and 12257 pulp (C).

HOOK
- Size K/10½ (6.5mm) crochet hook or any size to obtain gauge

GAUGE
- Rounds 1–2 in pattern = 2¾" (7cm)

Motif

Note: All rounds are worked on the right side.

With color A, ch 4; join with sl st to form ring.

ROUND 1: Ch 4, (counts as tr throughout) 15 tr in ring; join with sl st in top of beg ch-4, do not fasten off—16 tr.

ROUND 2: Ch 1, sc in same st; *ch 3, sk next st, sc in next st; rep from * 6 more times, ch 3; join with sl st in first sc—8 sc and 8 ch-3 sps. Fasten off.

ROUND 3: Join B with sl st in any ch-3 sp, ch 4, 4 tr in same sp; ch 1, sk next st; *5 tr in next ch-3 sp, ch 1, sk next st; rep from * 6 more times; join with sl st in top of beg ch-4—40 tr and 8 ch-1 sps. Fasten off.

ROUND 4: Join C with sc in any ch-1 sp, ch 3, sc in same sp; *sc in next 5 sts, (sc, ch 3, sc) in next ch-1 sp; rep from * 6 more times, sc in last 5 sts; join with sl st in first sc—56 sc and 8 ch-3 sps. Fasten off.

ROUND 5: Join color A with sl st in any ch-3 sp, ch 3 (counts as dc), 6 dc in same sp; *ch 1, sk next 3 sts, sc in next st, ch 1, sk next 3 sts, 7 dc in next ch-3 sp; rep from * 6 more times, ch 1, sk next 3 sts, sc in next st, ch 1, sk next 3 sts; join with sl st in top of beg ch-3—56 dc and 8 sc.

Finishing

Weave in all ends.

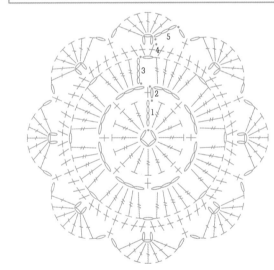

Mix and Match with these motifs:

Harvest Motif

Raspberry Tart Motif

Puddles Gather Rain Motif

Serene Motif

Scary Fun Motif

Granny Octagon
Skill level: Beginner | Finished measurement: 6½" (17cm) point to point

Take the granny square and make it edgy—really edgy—add four more edges! This is a fun way for a beginner to try a new shape.

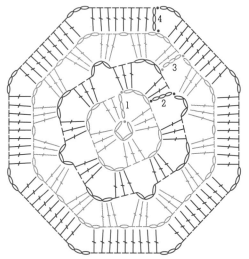

GETTING STARTED

YARN

• Worsted weight yarn in 3 different colors (A, B and C)

The motif shown at left was made using Red Heart Eco-Ways (70% acrylic, 30% recycled polyester, 4oz/113g balls/186yd/170m) in colors 3523 asparagus (A), 1615 lichen (B) and 3114 chamois (C).

HOOK

• Size K/10½ (6.5mm) crochet hook or any size to obtain gauge

GAUGE

• Rounds 1–2 in pattern = 3½" (9cm)

Motif

Note: All rounds are worked on the right side. On round 3, the ch-1 sp counts as a st.

With A, ch 4, join with sl st to form ring.

ROUND 1: Ch 3 (counts as dc), 2 dc in ring, ch 3; *3 dc in ring, ch 3; rep from * 2 more times; join with sl st in top of beg ch-3—12 dc, 4 ch-3 sp. Fasten off.

ROUND 2: Join B with sl st in any ch-3 sp, ch 3 (counts as dc), (2 dc, ch 3, 3 dc) in same sp; *ch 3, (3 dc, ch 3, 3 dc) in next ch-3 sp; rep from * 2 more times, ch 3; join with sl st in top of beg ch-3—24 dc, 8 ch-3 sps. Fasten off.

ROUND 3: Join C with sl st in any ch-3 sp, ch 3 (counts as dc) (2 dc, ch 3, 3 dc) in same sp; *ch 1, (3 dc, ch 3, 3 dc) in next ch-3 sp; rep from * 6 more times, ch 1; join with sl st in top of beg ch-3—48 dc, 8 ch-3 sps, 8 ch-1 sps. Fasten off.

ROUND 4: Join A with sl st in any ch-3 sp, ch 3 (counts as dc); *dc in each of next 7 sts, (dc, ch 3, dc) in ch-3 sp; rep from * 6 more times, dc in each of next 7 sts, (dc, ch 3) in ch-3 sp; join with sl st in top of beg ch-3—8 ch-3 sps, 72 dc. Fasten off.

Finishing

Weave in all ends.

Mix and Match with these motifs:

Pick a Posie Motif

Off Center Motif

Hurricane Motif

Gift Package Motif

Oro Sol Motif

Purple Sunset

Skill level: Beginner | Finished measurement: 6" (15cm) point to point

Our son named this pretty motif. He saw a purple sun in the middle and rays coming out from it. Who am I to argue? What do you see?

GETTING STARTED

YARN
- Worsted weight yarn in 2 different colors (A and B)

The motif shown at right was made using Louet Riverstone (100% wool, 3.5oz/100g hanks/193yd/176m) in colors 66 phantom (A) and 03 sachet (B).

HOOK
- Size K/10½ (6.5mm) crochet hook or any size to obtain gauge

GAUGE
- Rounds 1–2 in pattern = 3" (8cm)

Motif

Note: All rounds are worked on the right side.

With A, ch 4, join with sl st to form ring.

ROUND 1: Ch 1, 8 sc in ring; join with sl st in first sc, do not fasten off—8 sc.

ROUND 2: Ch 4 (counts as tr), tr in same st; *ch 2, 2 tr in next st; rep from * 6 more times, ch 2; join with sl st in top of beg ch-4—16 tr, 8 ch-2 sps. Fasten off.

ROUND 3: Join B with sl st in any ch-2 sp, ch 3 (counts as dc), dc in next 2 sts; * (dc, ch 3, dc) in ch-2 sp, dc in each of next 2 sts; rep from * 6 more times, dc in ch-2 sp, ch 3; join with sl st in top of beg ch-3—32 dc, 8 ch-3 sps. Fasten off.

ROUND 4: Join A with sc in any ch-3 corner sp, 4 more sc in same sp; *ch 1, sk 1 st, sc in each of next 2 sts, ch 1, sk 1 st**, 5 sc in ch-3 sp; rep from * 6 more times rep from * to ** once; join with sl st in first sc, do not fasten off—56 sc, 16 ch-1 sps.

ROUND 5: Ch 1, sc in same st, sc in next st; *3 sc in next st, sc in each of next 2 sts, sc in ch-1 sp, ch 3, sk 2 sts, sc in ch-1 sp**, sc in each of next 2 sts; rep from * 6 more times; rep from * to ** once; join with sl st in first sc—8 ch-3 sps, 72 sc. Fasten off.

Finishing

Weave in all ends.

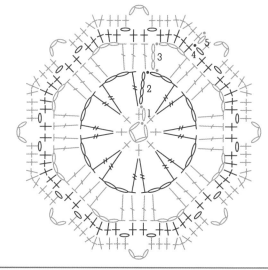

Mix and Match with these motifs:

Octagon Medallion Motif

Polka Dot Motif

Wrought Iron Motif

Whimsy Motif

Chair Back Motif

Purple Pansy
Skill level: Easy | Finished measurement: 6" (15cm) side to side

The purple pansy was our troop flower when I was a Girl Scout years ago—a quaint tradition of a bygone era.

GETTING STARTED

YARN

• Worsted weight yarn in 3 different colors (A, B and C)

The motif shown at left was made using Caron Simply Soft (100% acrylic, 6oz/170g balls/315yd/288m) in colors 9712 soft blue (A), 9726 soft yellow (B) and 9738 violet (C).

HOOK

• Size K/10½ (6.5mm) crochet hook or any size to obtain gauge

GAUGE

• Round 1 in pattern = 2¼" (6cm)

Motif

Note: All rounds are worked on the right side.

With A, ch 5; join with sl st to form ring.

ROUND 1: Beg-cl in ring, (ch 2, cl) in ring 7 times, ch 2; join with sl st in top of beg-cl—8 cl, 8 ch-2 sps. Fasten off.

ROUND 2: Join B with sl st in any ch-2 sp, ch 3 (counts as dc), 2 dc in same st; *ch 2, sk 1 cl, 3 dc in ch-2 sp; rep from * 6 more times, ch 2; join with sl st in top of beg ch-3—24 dc, 8 ch-2 sps. Fasten off.

ROUND 3: Join C with sc in any ch-2 sp, (ch 2, sc) in same sp; *sc in each of next 3 sts, (sc, ch 2, sc) in ch-2 sp; rep from * 6 more times; join with sl st in first sc—8 ch-2 sps, 40 sc. Fasten off.

ROUND 4: Join A with sl st in any ch-2 sp, ch 3 (counts as dc), 2 dc in same sp; *ch 2, FPdc in middle dc of 3-dc group in round 2, ch 2**, 3 dc in next ch-2 sp; rep from * 6 more times; rep from * to ** 1 time; join with sl st in top of beg ch-3, do not fasten off—24 dc, 8 FPdc, 16 ch-2 sps.

ROUND 5: Ch 1, sc in same st; *3 sc in next st, sc in next st, 3 hdc in ch-2 sp, hdc in next st, 3 hdc in ch-2 sp**, sc in next st; rep from * 6 more times; rep from * to ** 1 time; join with sl st in first sc—56 hdc, 40 sc. Fasten off.

Finishing

Weave in all ends.

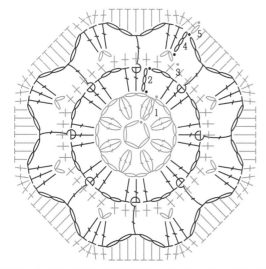

Mix and Match with these motifs:

Oscar Square Motif

Rose Octagon Motif

Bluebonnet Motif

Cameo Motif

Simplicity Motif

Octagon Medallion
Skill level: Intermediate | Finished measurement: 7" (18cm) side to side

This should be a pattern for china dishware. Can you see it?

GETTING STARTED

YARN

• Worsted weight yarn in 3 different colors (A, B and C)

The motif shown at right was made using Red Heart Super Saver (100% acrylic, 7oz/198g balls/364yd/333m) in color 0528 medium purple (A); TLC Essentials (100% acrylic, 6oz/170g balls/312yd/285m) in color 2101 white (B); TLC Essentials (100% acrylic, 4.5oz/127g balls/245yd/224m) in color 2948 blue jean (C).

HOOK

• Size K/10½ (6.5mm) crochet hook or any size to obtain gauge

GAUGE

• Rounds 1–4 in pattern = 4¼" (11cm)

Motif

Note: All rounds are worked on the right side.

With color A, ch 4; join with sl st to form ring.

ROUND 1: Ch 1, 8 sc in ring; join with sl st in first sc, do not fasten off—8 sc.

ROUND 2: *Ch 7, sl st in same st, sl st in next st; repeat from * 7 more times; no need to join—8 ch-7 sps; 16 sl sts. Fasten off.

ROUND 3: Join B with sc in any ch-7 sp; *ch 5, sc in next ch-7 sp; rep from * 6 more times, ch 5; join with sl st in first sc, do not fasten off—8 sc, 8 ch-5 sps.

ROUND 4: Ch 1, sc in same st; *(2 sc, ch 3, 2 sc) in next ch-5 sp, sc in next sc; rep from * 6 more times, (2 sc, ch 3, 2 sc) in ch-5 sp; join with sl st in first sc—40 sc, 8 ch-3 sps. Fasten off.

ROUND 5: Join C with sl st in any ch-3 sp, ch 3 (counts as first dc), 4 dc in same sp, ch 3, sk 5 sts; *5 dc in ch-3 sp, ch 3, sk 5 sts; rep from * 6 more times; join with sl st in top beg ch-3—40 dc, 8 ch-3 sps. Fasten off.

ROUND 6: Join A with sc in 3rd dc of 5-dc group, 2 sc in same st; *ch 2, sk 2 sts, working over the top of the ch-3 sp and working into the middle st of the 5-sc group on round 4, dc in center sc on round 4, ch 2, sk 2 sts on current round**; 3 sc in next dc; rep from * 6 more times; rep from * to ** once; join with sl st in first sc—8 dc, 16 ch-2 sps, 24 sc. Fasten off.

ROUND 7: Join C with sc in middle sc of 3-sc corner, 2 more sc in same st; *sc in next st, 3 sc in ch-2 sp, sc in next st, 3 sc in ch-2 sp, sc in next st**, 3 sc in next st; rep from * 6 more times; rep from * to ** once; join with sl st in first sc—96 sc. Fasten off.

Finishing

Weave in all ends.

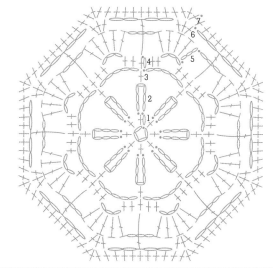

85

Mix and Match with these motifs:

Try-It Triangle Motif

Red Light, Green Light Motif

Golden Hexagon Motif

Cherry Cordial Motif

Acapulco Motif

Floral Octagon
Skill level: Intermediate | Finished measurement: 6¼" (16cm) point to point

Like a tiny rosebud on calico fabric, this flowery octagon is tickled pink. Put a field of these together and you'll make the day of any little rosebud.

GETTING STARTED

YARN
- Worsted weight yarn in 3 different colors (A, B and C)

The motif shown at left was made using Universal Yarns Classic Worsted (80% Acrylic, 20% Wool, 3.5oz/100g balls/197yd/180m) in colors 615 bubblegum (A), 616 pink (B) and 614 light pink (C).

HOOK
- Size K/10½ (6.5mm) crochet hook or any size to obtain gauge

GAUGE
- Rounds 1–2 in pattern = 3¼" (8cm)

SPECIAL STITCHES
- FPdc = Front Post double crochet

Motif

Note: All rounds are worked on the right side.

With A, ch 4, join with sl st to form ring.

ROUND 1: Ch 1, 8 sc in ring; join with sl st in first sc, do not fasten off—8 sc

ROUND 2: Ch 7 (counts as tr plus ch 3); *tr in next sc, ch 3; rep from * 6 more times; join with sl st in 4th ch of beg ch-7—8 tr, 8 ch-3 sps. Fasten off.

ROUND 3: Join B with sl st in any ch-3 sp, ch 3 (counts as dc), (dc, ch 3, 2 dc) in same sp; *FPdc around next st, (2 dc, ch 3, 2 dc) in next sp; rep from * 6 more times, FPdc around next st; join with sl st in top beg ch-3—32 dc, 8 FPdc. Fasten off.

ROUND 4 (Join Round): The second and all other motifs made can be joined on this round.

FIRST MOTIF: Join C with sl st in any ch-3 corner, ch 3 (counts as dc), 8 more dc in same sp; *sk 2 dc, sc in next st, sk 2 dc, 9 dc in ch-3 sp; rep from * 6 more times, sk 2 dc, sc in next st, sk 2 dc; join with sl st in top beg ch-3—8 sc, 72 dc. Fasten off.

SECOND AND ALL SUBSEQUENT MOTIFS: Take care to join in middle of all adjacent dc-9 groups. Join C with sl st in any ch-3 corner, ch 3 (counts as dc), 8 more dc in same sp; *sk 2 dc, sc in next st, sk 2 dc, 4 dc in ch-3 sp, sl st in middle dc of dc-9 group on another motif, 5 dc in same ch-3 sp; rep from * once, **sk 2 dc, sc in next st, sk 2 dc, 9 dc in ch-3 sp; rep from ** 4 more times, sk 2 dc, sc in next st, sk 2 dc; join with sl st in top beg ch-3—8 sc, 72 dc. Fasten off.

Finishing

Weave in all ends.

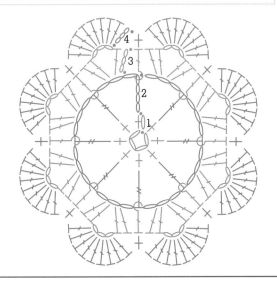

Mix and Match with these motifs:

Oro Sol Motif

Purple Pansy Motif

Cameo Motif

Chair Back Motif

Harvest Motif

Drama Queen

Skill level: Intermediate | Finished measurement: 5½" (14cm) side to side

Is there anything more formal than gold on black? All dressed up and ready to go, this motif reminds me of an elegant night out.

GETTING STARTED

YARN

• Worsted weight yarn in 3 different colors (A, B and C)

The motif shown at right was made using Caron Simply Soft (100% acrylic, 6oz/170g balls/315yd/288m) in colors 9703 bone (A), 9727 black (B) and 9726 soft yellow (C).

HOOK

• Size K/10½ (6.5mm) crochet hook or any size to obtain gauge

GAUGE

• Rounds 1–2 in pattern = 3" (8cm)

Motif

Note: All rounds are worked on the right side.

With A, ch 5; join with sl st to form ring.

ROUND 1: Ch 1, 8 sc in ring; join with sl st in first sc, do not fasten off—8 sc.

ROUND 2: *Ch 7, sl st in 6th ch from hook, sl st in next ch, sl st in same sc and sl st in next sc; rep from * 7 more times; no need to join—8 ch-7 loops. Fasten off.

ROUND 3: Join B with sc in any ch-7 loop of round 2; *ch 3, sc in next loop; rep from * 6 more times; ch 3; join with sl st in first sc, do not fasten off—8 sc, 8 ch-3 sps.

ROUND 4: Ch 3 (counts as dc); *4 dc in ch-3 sp, dc in next st; rep from 6 more times, 4 dc in next ch-3 sp; join with sl st in top of beg ch-3—40 dc. Fasten off.

ROUND 5: Join C with sc in a dc above any ch-7 loop, 2 more sc in same st; *sc in each of next 4 sts, 3 sc in next st; rep from * 6 more times, sc in each of next 4 sts; join with sl st in first sc—56 sc. Fasten off.

ROUND 6: Join B with sl st in middle sc of any 3-sc corner, ch 2 (counts as hdc), (hdc, dc, 2 hdc) in same st; *sk next 2 sts, sc in each of next 2 sts, sk next 2 sts, (2 hdc, dc, 2 hdc) in next st; rep from * 6 more times; sk next 2 sts, sc in each of next 2 sts, sk next 2 sts; join with sl st in top of beg ch-2—32 hdc, 8 dc, 16 sc. Fasten off.

Finishing

Weave in all ends.

87

Mix and Match with these motifs:

Floral Octagon Motif

Twinkle Motif

Campfire Motif

Puddles Gather Rain Motif

Vintage Motif

Red Light, Green Light

Skill level: Intermediate

Finished measurement: 6½" (17cm) side to side

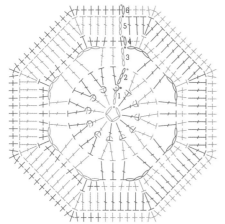

Mix and Match with these motifs:

Campfire Motif

South Beach Motif

Oro Sol Motif

Purple Pansy Motif

Beveled Motif

Inspired by the children's game, this motif changes colors in mid-round!

GETTING STARTED

YARN

- Worsted weight yarn in 2 different colors (A and B)

The motif shown at left was made using Universal Yarns Deluxe Worsted (100% wool, 3.5oz/100g balls/220yd/200m) in colors 3620 coral (A) and 12183 city turf (B).

HOOK

- Size K/10½ (6.5mm) crochet hook or any size to obtain gauge

GAUGE

- Rounds 1–2 in pattern = 2½" (6cm)

Motif

Note: All rounds are worked on the right side. Colors are changed in the middle of the round—drop the unused color and work over it until it is needed again.

With A, ch 4, join with sl st to form ring.

ROUND 1: With A, ch 3 (counts as dc here and throughout), 5 dc in ring, switching to B in last st, with B, 6 dc in ring; join with sl st in top of beg ch-3, do not fasten off—12 dc.

ROUND 2: Continue using B, ch 3, FPdc around same st; *dc in next st, FPdc around same st**; rep from * to ** 4 more times, switching to A in last st, with A rep from * to ** 6 times; join with sl st in top of beg ch-3, do not fasten off—12 dc, 12 FPdc.

ROUND 3: Continue using A, ch 3, dc in each of next 2 sts; *ch 3, dc in each of next 3 sts; rep from * 2 more times, ch 3, switching to B in last ch, with B; **dc in each of next 3 sts, ch 3; rep from ** 3 more times, ch 3; join with sl st in top of beg ch-3, do not fasten off—24 dc, 8 ch-3 sps.

ROUND 4: Continue using B, ch 1, sc in same st, sc in each of next 2 sts, (2 sc, hdc, 2 sc) in next ch-3 sp; *sc in each of next 3 sts, (2 sc, hdc, 2 sc) in next ch-3 sp**; rep from * to ** 2 more times, (2 sc, hdc, 2 sc) in next ch-3 sp, switching to A in last st, with A, rep from * to ** 4 times; join with sl st in first sc, do not fasten off—56 sc, 8 hdc.

ROUND 5: Continue using A, ch 3, dc in each of next 4 sts, 3 dc in next st; *dc in each of next 7 sts, 3 dc in next st**; rep from * to ** 2 more times, dc in each of next 2 sts, switching to B in last st, with B, dc in each of next 5 sts, 3 dc in next st; rep from * to ** 3 more times, dc in each of last 2 sts; join with sl st in top of beg ch-3, do not fasten off—80 dc.

ROUND 6: Continue using B, ch 1, sc in same st, sc in each of next 5 sts, 3 sc in next st; *sc in each of next 9 sts, 3 sc in next st**; rep from * to ** 2 more times, sc in each of next 3 sts, switching to A in last st, with A, sc in each of next 6 sts, 3 sc in next st, rep from * to ** 3 more times, sc in each of last 3 sts; join with sl st in first sc, do not fasten off—96 sc.

Finishing

Weave in all ends.

The colors and popcorn stitches make me think of a mouthwatering berry pastry.

Raspberry Tart
Skill level: Advanced
Finished measurement: 6" (15cm) side to side

GETTING STARTED

YARN
• Worsted weight yarn in 2 different colors (A and B)

The motif shown at right was made using Bernat Satin (100% acrylic, 3.5oz/100g balls/163yd/149m) in colors 04309 lavender (A) and 04531 rouge (B).

HOOK
• Size K/10½ (6.5mm) crochet hook or any size to obtain gauge

GAUGE
• Rounds 1–2 in pattern 3" (8cm)

SPECIAL STITCHES
• pop = popcorn (5 dc)

Motif

Note: All rounds are worked on the right side.

With A, ch 6; join with sl st to form ring.

ROUND 1: Ch 1, 16 sc in ring; join with sl st in first sc, do not fasten off—16 sc.

ROUND 2: Ch 7 (counts as tr plus 3 ch), sk 1 st; *tr in next st, ch 3, sk 1 st; rep from * 6 more times; join with sl st in 4th ch of beg ch-7—8 tr, 8 ch-3 sps. Fasten off.

ROUND 3: Join B with sc in any tr, ch 3, sc in same st; *sc in next ch-3 sp, working behind round 2, pop in skipped sc on round 1, sc in same ch-3 sp**, (sc, ch 3, sc) in next tr; rep from * 6 more times; rep from * to ** once; join with sl st in first sc, do not fasten off—8 pop, 32 sc, 8 ch-3 sps.

ROUND 4: Sl st into next ch-3 sp, ch 1, sc in same sp, ch 7, sk 5 sts; *sc in next ch-3 sp, ch 7, sk 5 sts; rep from * 6 more times; join with sl st in first sc, do not fasten off—8 sc, 8 ch-7 sps.

ROUND 5: Ch 1, 3 sc in same st, 7 sc in ch-7 sp; *3 sc in next st, 7 sc in ch-7 sp; rep from * 6 more times; join with sl st in first sc, do not fasten off—80 sc.

ROUND 6: Ch 1; *3 sc in next st, sl st in next 9 sts; rep from * 8 times; join with sl st in first sc—24 sc, 72 sl st. Fasten off.

Finishing

Weave in all ends.

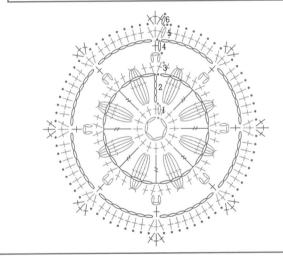

Mix and Match with these motifs:

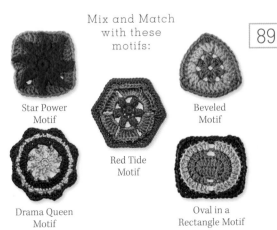

Star Power Motif

Drama Queen Motif

Red Tide Motif

Beveled Motif

Oval in a Rectangle Motif

89

Afghans on the Go

Now that you have made a bunch of beautiful motifs, I'm sure you're ready to make a full blanket! This chapter contains ten afghan patterns that you can use as a jumping-off point to create your own designs and layouts.

A project composed of just one motif can be stunning, like two of the projects in this chapter: *Flowers Galore* and *Trillions of Triangles*. Don't just look at the motifs themselves; pay attention to the spaces between motifs and the shadows cast by dimensional stitches. You may find a complexity that you didn't see at first. One-motif projects don't have to be repetitious. Change up the colors or use scrap yarn for variety.

Don't stop there, though. Bump up the visual impact by mixing two motifs of the same or different shapes. Create harmony through the color scheme, and add variety with the different stitches and textures. Use symmetry in the layout by using a checkerboard pattern, or place motifs at random to give your blanket a fun and spontaneous feel. *Reflected Sunlight*, *Blueberry Pancakes*, *Yours Truly* and *Brilliant Starburst* are a few of my two-motif designs. I know you'll have as much fun creating your own designs as I did.

Finally, go wild with multiple shapes and motifs! My *Spring Octagons*, *French Country* and *Ocean's Tide* blankets use some of my favorite motifs, and *All Call* uses all of the motifs shown in the book.

With fifty interchangeable motifs and unlimited color choices, the possibilities are endless. Every project you create will truly be one-of-a-kind!

91

Reflected Sunlight

Skill level: Easy | Finished measurement: 47" × 61" (119cm × 155cm)

When you combine a motif named Oro Sol, Spanish
for "golden sun," with the Puddles Gather Rain motif,
you get a stunning mosaic of color and depth—like sun
reflected in the water. An easy join-as-you-go technique
makes the assembly quick and simple.

GETTING STARTED

YARN

• Worsted weight yarn in 3 different colors (A,
B and C)

*The project shown was made using Universal
Yarns Deluxe Worsted (100% wool, 3.5oz/100g
balls/220yd/200m) with 6 skeins of color 12204
pussywillow gray (A), 5 skeins of color 41795 nectarine (B) and 2 skeins of color 12257 pulp (C).*

HOOK

• Size K/10½ (6.5mm) crochet hook or any
size to obtain gauge

NOTIONS

• Yarn needle

GAUGE

• Octagons: Rounds 1–2 in pattern = 2¾"
(7cm)

• Squares: Rounds 1–2 in pattern = 2" (6cm)

Note: All rounds are worked on the right side.

Motif A: Oro Sol

Make 63.

With color A, ch 4, join with sl st to form ring.

ROUND 1: Ch 4, (counts as tr throughout) 15 tr in ring; join with sl st in top of beg ch-4—16 tr.

ROUND 2: Ch 1, sc in same st; *ch 3, skip next st, sc in next st; rep from * 6 more times, ch 3; join with sl st in first sc—8 sc and 8 ch-3 sps. Fasten off.

ROUND 3: Join B with sl st in any ch-3 sp, ch 4, 4 tr in same sp, ch 1, skip next st; *5 tr in next ch-3 sp, ch 1, skip next st; rep from * 6 more times; join with sl st in top of beg ch-4—40 tr and 8 ch-1 sps. Fasten off.

ROUND 4: Join C with sc in any ch-1 sp, ch 3, sc in same sp; *sc in next 5 sts, (sc, ch 3, sc) in next ch-1 sp; rep from * 6 more times, sc in last 5 sts; join with sl st in first sc-56 sc and 8 ch-3 sps. Fasten off.

JOINING ROUND: Lay out octagons in 7 rows of 9. Work round 5, using stitch diagram and assembly diagram for assistance, work connecting petals as follows: In this case, a petal is defined as a 7-dc group.

FIRST MOTIF (not joined to any other) Round 5: Join A with sl st in any ch-3 sp, ch 3 (counts as dc), 6 dc in same sp; *ch 1, skip next 3 sts, sc in next st, ch 1, skip next 3 sts, 7 dc in next ch-3 sp; rep from * 6 more times, ch 1, skip next 3 sts, sc in next st, ch 1, skip next 3 sts; join with sl st in top of beg ch-3—56 dc and 8 sc.

Subsequent motifs (joined on two petals of every adjacent octagon): Take care to join on every dc-7 group necessary.

ROUND 5: Join A with sl st in any ch-3 sp, ch 3 (counts as dc), 6 dc in same sp; *ch 1, skip next 3 sts, sc in next st, ch 1, skip next 3 sts, 4 dc in ch-3 sp, sl st in middle dc of adjacent petal on second motif, 3 dc in same ch-3 sp; rep from * twice on each adjacent octagon, **ch 1, skip next 3 sts, sc in next st, ch 1, skip next 3 sts, 7 dc in next ch-3 sp; rep from ** around, ch 1, skip next 3 sts, sc in next st, ch 1, skip next 3 sts; join with sl st in top of beg-ch—56 dc and 8 sc.

Motif B: Puddles Gather Rain Square

Make 48.

With B, ch 4.

ROUND 1: 7 dc in the 4th ch from hook; join with sl st in 4th ch of beg ch-4—8 dc. Fasten off.

ROUND 2: Join A with sl st in any st, ch 4 (counts as tr), 2 tr in same st; 3 tr in each of next 7 sts; join with sl st in top of beg ch-4—24 tr. Fasten off.

After all the octagons are joined to one another, all square inserts are added and joined to 4 octagons (see Assembly Diagram) Round 3: Join B with sc in any st; ch 2, sl st in join where two octagons come together; *ch 2, sk 2 sts on round 2, sc in next st on insert motif, ch 5, sk 2 sts**, sc in next st; rep from * around, ending last rep at **; join with sl st in first sc—8 sc, 4 ch-5 sps, 4 joined corners. Fasten off.

Edging

ROUND 1: Join A with sc in any st, sc in every st and ch-1 sp around; join with sl st in first sc—892 sc. Fasten off.

Finishing

Weave in all ends.

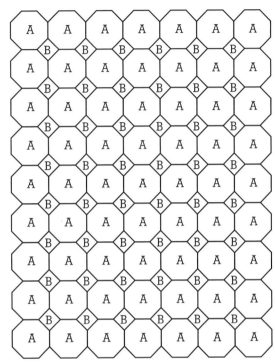

Assembly Diagram

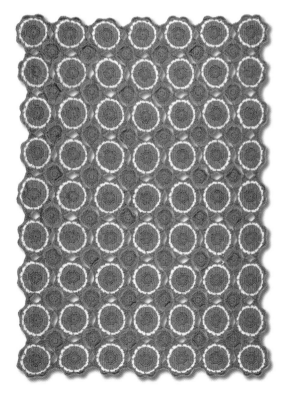

Trillions of Triangles
Skill level: Easy | Finished measurement: 34½" × 57" (88cm × 145cm)

Triangles make great optical illusions. It is easy to
see the individual triangles as well as the hexagons
and diamonds the sets of triangles make up. What a
stunning result for such a simple project!

GETTING STARTED

YARN
• Worsted weight yarn in 3 different colors (A,
B and C)

*The project shown was made using Spud &
Chloe, Sweater (55% superwash wool, 45%
organic cotton, 3.5oz/100g hanks/160yd/146m)
with 5 hanks of color 7509 firecracker (A), 6
hanks of color 7506 toast (B) and 6 hanks of
color 7504 lake (C).*

HOOK
• Size K/10½ (6.5mm) crochet hook or any
size to obtain gauge

NOTIONS
• Yarn needle

GAUGE
• Motif Rounds 1–3 in pattern = 4" (10cm)

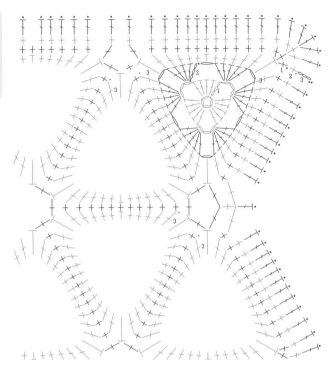

SPECIAL STITCHES

- sc2tog = single crochet decrease
- sc3tog = single crochet 3 together: [Insert hook in next st, yo, draw yarn through st] 3 times, yo, draw yarn through 4 loops on hook

Note: All rounds are worked on the right side.

Try-It Triangle Motif

Make 192 (8 rows of 24 triangles).

With A, ch 4, join with sl st to form ring.

ROUND 1: Ch 3 (counts as dc), 4 dc in ring; *ch 3, 5 dc in ring, rep from * once, ch 3; join with sl st in top of beg ch-3—15 dc, 3 ch-3 sps. Fasten off.

ROUND 2: Join B with sl st in first ch of any ch-3 corner, ch 3 (counts as dc), 4 more dc in same st, ch 1, sk 1 ch, 5 dc in next ch, ch 1, sk 5 sts; *5 dc in next ch, ch 1, sk 1 ch, 5 dc in next ch, ch 1, sk 5 dc; rep from * once; join with sl st in top of beg ch-3—30 dc, 6 ch-1 sps. Fasten off.

ROUND 3: Join C with sc in first st after any ch-1 corner, sc in next 4 dc, hdc in ch-1 sp; *sc in next 5 dc, hdc in ch-1 sp; rep from * 4 times; join with sl st in first sc—30 sc, 6 hdc. Fasten off.

Assembly

Assemble motifs into 8 rows of 24 triangles. With RS facing each other and C, matching stitches, sc through both thicknesses.

Edging

ROUND 1: Join C with sc in either corner, beginning a long side, 2 more sc in same st, *sc in each st across to next corner, 3 sc in middle st of corner, working along short side, sc in each st across, when you reach a "low point" where the motifs come together, sc2tog binding the two motifs together*, 3 sc in middle sc at next corner; rep from * to * once; join with sl st in first sc. Fasten off.

ROUND 2: Join A with sc where previously fastened off, 3 sc in middle sc of 3-sc corner, sc in each st across to next corner, 3 sc in middle sc of 3-sc corner, working across short side, sc in each st across, at the "low points" where motifs come together, sc3tog across 3 sts, 3 sc in middle sc at next corner; join with sl st in first sc—do not fasten off.

ROUND 3: Ch 3 (counts as dc), dc in next st, *3 dc in middle sc of 3-sc corner, dc in each st to next corner at the end of the side; rep from * around, working no dec at "low points"; join with sl st in top of beg ch-3, do not fasten off.

ROUND 4: Sl st in each st around; join with sl st in first st. Fasten off.

Finishing

Weave in all ends.

Edging Stitch Diagram

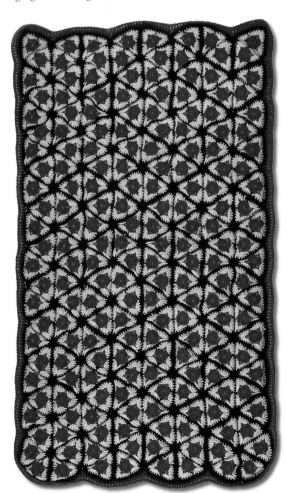

Blueberry Pancakes

Skill level: Easy | Finished measurement: 47"× 61" (119cm × 155cm)

Nothing says a leisurely morning like eating blueberry pancakes under a bright morning sky. Recapture that cozy feeling anytime wrapped up in a blanket that's bursting with bright color and warmth.

GETTING STARTED

YARN

• Worsted weight yarn in 3 different colors (A, B and C)

The project shown was made using Red Heart Super Saver (100% acrylic, 7oz/198g balls/ 364yd/333m) with 3 skeins of color 385 royal (A); Red Heart Kids (100% acrylic, 5oz/140g balls/290yd/265m) with 4 skeins of color 2650 pistachio (B); TLC Essentials (100% acrylic, 6oz/170g balls/312yd/285m) with 2 skeins of color 2690 fusion (C).

HOOK

• Size K/10½ (6.5mm) crochet hook or any size to obtain gauge

NOTIONS

• Yarn needle
• Stitch markers

GAUGE

• Rectangle: Rounds 1–2 in pattern = 3" × 3½" (8cm × 9cm)

Notes: All rounds are worked on the right side.

Motif A: Last Blueberry

Make 65.

With A, ch 6, join with sl st to form ring.

ROUND 1: Beg-cl in ring, ch 3, (cl, ch 3) in ring; (cl, ch 2) in ring, (cl, ch 3) 2 times in ring, (cl, ch 2) in ring; join with sl st in top of beg-cl—6 cl—4 ch-3 sps, 2 ch-2 sps. Fasten off.

ROUND 2: Join B with sl st in any ch-3 sp before a ch-2 sp, (beg-cl, ch 3, cl) in same sp, ch 1, sk cl, cl in next ch-2 sp, ch 1, (cl, ch 3, cl) in next ch-3 sp, ch 1, (cl, ch 3, cl) in next ch-3 sp, ch 1, cl in ch-2 sp, ch 1, (cl, ch 3, cl) in next ch-3 sp, ch 1; join with sl st in top beg-cl—10 cl, 4 ch-3 sps, 6 ch-1 sps. Fasten off.

ROUND 3: Join C with sc in ch-3 sp before a long side (with 2 ch-1 sps), (sc, dtr between clusters of round 1 into beg ch-6 ring, 2 sc) in same sp; *sc in next cl, [2 sc in next ch-1 sp, sc in next cl] twice, (2 sc, dtr between clusters of round 1 into beg ch-6 ring, 2 sc) in next ch-3 sp, 2 sc in next cl, sc in ch-1 sp, 2 sc in next cl*; (2 sc, dtr between clusters of round 1 into beg ch-6 ring, 2 sc) in next ch-3 sp; rep from * to * once; join with sl st in first sc—4 dtr, 40 sc. Fasten off.

ROUND 4: Working in blps only; join A with sc in dtr of a corner before either long side, 2 more sc in same st, sc in each of next 11 sts, 3 sc in next st, sc in next 9 sts, 3 sc in next st, sc in next 11 sts, 3 sc in next st, sc in next 9 sts; join with sl st in first sc—52 sc. Fasten off.

Motif B: Oscar Square

Make 65.

With B, ch 4, join with sl st to form ring.

ROUND 1: Ch 3 (counts as dc), dc in ring, ch 3, *2 dc in ring, ch 3; rep from * 3 times; join with sl st in top of beg-ch, do not fasten off—8 dc and 4 ch-3 sp.

ROUND 2: Sl st in next st, *ch 2, 8 dc in next ch-3 sp, ch 2, sl st in each of next 2 sts; rep from * 4 times omitting last sl st; join with sl st in first st—32 dc, 8 sl st and 8 ch-2 sps. Fasten off.

ROUND 3: Join B with sc in blp of first dc of any 8-dc group, sc in next 3 sts, ch 3, sc in next 4 sts, skip sl sts and ch-sps; *ch 1, sc in next 4 sts, ch 3, sc in next 4 sts; rep from * 2 more times, ch 1, skip sl sts and ch-sps; join with sl st in first sc, do not fasten off—32 sc, 4 ch-1 sps and 4 ch-3 sp.

ROUND 4: Ch 1, working in both loops of sts, sc in each of next 4 sts; *3 sc in ch-3 sp, sc in each of next 9 sts; rep from * 2 more times, 3 sc in ch-3 sp, sc in each of last 5 sts; join with sl st in top of first sc—48 sc. Fasten off.

Assembly

Must assemble in multiples of 2 across.

Place markers every two motifs so that they line up when assembling.

In this project the placement is a checkerboard, but because the rectangle is 2 stitches longer than it is wide, assembly requires a little more strategy. In this case, with yarn needle and A, whipstitch with wrong sides together, through outer loops only, the short side of a rectangle to any side of a square.

Make 65 pairs.

When all the pairs are made, whipstitch 13 pairs into a column.

Whipstitch the 5 columns together.

B	A	B	A	B	A	B	A	B	A
A	B	A	B	A	B	A	B	A	B
B	A	B	A	B	A	B	A	B	A
A	B	A	B	A	B	A	B	A	B
B	A	B	A	B	A	B	A	B	A
A	B	A	B	A	B	A	B	A	B
B	A	B	A	B	A	B	A	B	A
A	B	A	B	A	B	A	B	A	B
B	A	B	A	B	A	B	A	B	A
A	B	A	B	A	B	A	B	A	B
B	A	B	A	B	A	B	A	B	A
A	B	A	B	A	B	A	B	A	B
B	A	B	A	B	A	B	A	B	A

Assembly Diagram

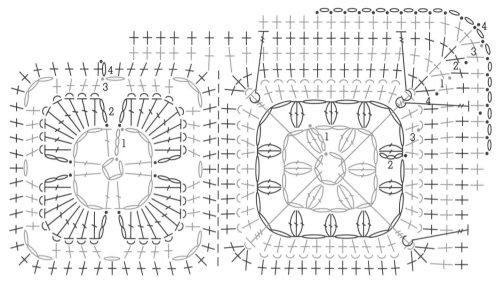

Edging Stitch Diagram

Edging

ROUND 1: Join A with sc in middle sc of corner beginning a short side where a rectangle is on the corner, 2 sc in same st; *sc in each st across to next corner, (including the middle sc of each motif)**, 3 sc in middle sc of next 3-sc corner; rep from * around, ending last rep at **; join with sl st in first sc—622 sc. Fasten off.

ROUND 2: Join C with sc in middle sc of sc-3 corner beginning a short side, 2 sc in same st, sc in each of next 2 sts; *FPtr around FPdtr of motif directly below it, skip st behind FPtr just made, sc in each of next 9 sts, FPtr around next FPdtr in motif directly below, skip st behind FPtr just made, sc in each of next 17 sts*; rep from 1st * across to last 15 sts before corner, sc in each of last 15 sts, 3 sc in next st, sc in each of next 15 sts; **FPtr around next FPdtr, skip st behind FPtr just made, sc in each of next 7 sts, FPtr around next FPdtr, skip st behind FPtr just made, sc in each of next 17 sts**; rep from ** to ** across to last 15 sts before the corner, sc in each of the last 15 sts, 3 sc in next st, sc in each of next 15 sts; ; rep from * to * last 2 sts before the corner, sc in each of last 2 sts, 3 sc in next st, sc in each 2 sts; rep from ** to ** across to last 2 sts, sc in each of last 2 sts; join with sl st in first sc—630 sts. Fasten off.

ROUND 3: Join B with sc in middle sc of any 3-sc corner, 2 sc in same st; *sc in each st to next corner**, 3 sc in middle sc of sc-3 corner; rep from * around, ending last rep at **; join with sl st in first sc—638 sc. Fasten off.

ROUND 4: Join A with sl st in middle sc of any 3-sc corner, ch 1; (sl st, ch 1) in each st around; join with sl st in first sl st—638 sl sts, 638 ch-1 spaces. Fasten off.

Finishing

Weave in all ends.

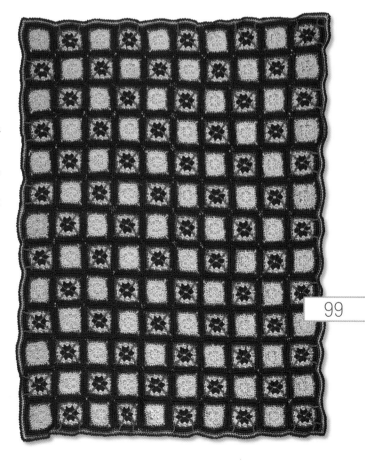

99

Flowers Galore
Skill level: Intermediate | Finished measurement: 44" × 57½" (112cm × 146cm)

Like a perfectly manicured garden, this patch of flowers reflects sunshine and blue skies. This pattern would be perfect for using scraps and creating a wildflower effect. Replace all the orange with multiple colors and choose one main color to unify the entire project and voilà—your own unique flower patch.

100

GETTING STARTED

YARN
• Worsted weight yarn in 2 different colors (A and B)

The project shown was made using TLC Essentials (100% acrylic, 6oz/170g balls/312yd/285m) with 5 skeins in color 2820 robin egg (A); Red Heart Super Saver (100% acrylic,7oz/198g balls/364yd/333m) with 4 skeins in color 256 carrot (B).

HOOK
• Size K/10½ (6.5mm) crochet hook or any size to obtain gauge

NOTIONS
• Yarn needle

GAUGE
• Motif Rounds 1–2 in pattern = 3½" (9cm)

Note: All rounds are worked on the right side.

Flower Patch Motif

Make 130.

With A, ch 3, join with sl st to form ring.

ROUND 1: (Ch 4, sl st) 4 times in ring; join with sl st in first sl st—4 ch-4 sps, 4 sl sts. Fasten off.

ROUND 2: Join B with sl st in any ch-4 sp, (beg tr-cl, ch 3, tr-cl in same sp), ch 3; *(tr-cl, ch 3, tr-cl) in next ch-3 sp, ch 3; rep from * 2 more times; join with sl st in top of beg-cl—8 tr-cl, 8 ch-3 sps. Fasten off.

ROUND 3: Join A with sc in cl where previously fastened off; *3 sc in ch-3 sp, sc in next cl, (2 sc, hdc, 2 sc) in next ch-3 sp**, sc in next cl; rep from * 2 more times; rep from * to ** once; join with sl st in first sc, do not fasten off—4 hdc, 36 sc.

ROUND 4: Ch 1, sc in same st, sc in next 6 sts; *3 sc in next st, sc in next 9 sc; rep from * 2 more times, 3 sc in next sc, sc in last 2 sts; join with sl st in first sc—48 sc. Fasten off.

Assembly

With A and yarn needle, arrange motifs into 10 columns of 13 squares, with RS facing each other. Sewing through outer loops only, matching stitches, whipstitch motifs together.

Edging

ROUND 1: With A, join in back loop only of middle sc of 3-sc corner beginning a short side, 2 more sc in same st, *work 128 sc evenly spaced across short side, 3 sc in middle sc of 3-sc corner, work 167 sc evenly spaced across long side**, 3 sc in middle sc of 3-sc corner, rep from * to ** once, join with sl st in first sc, do not fasten off—602 sc.

ROUND 2: Ch 1, sc in same st, ch 3, sk 1 st, *sc in next st, ch 2, sk 2 sts*; rep from * to * 43 times, **sc in next st, ch 3, sk 1 st for corner**; rep from * to * 57 times; rep from ** to ** once; rep from * to * 42 times; rep from ** to ** once; rep from * to * 56 times, join with sl st in first sc—4 ch-3 corner sps, 200 ch-2 sps. Fasten off.

ROUND 3: Join B with sc in sc before any corner, *ch 1, working behind ch-3 sp in round 2, (dc, ch 1, dc, ch 1, dc) in next unused sc in round 1, ch 1, sc in next st in round 2, (ch 1, working behind the ch-2 sp, dc2tog in the next 2 unused sts in round 1, ch 1, sc in next st in round 2) across side to next corner; rep from * around, omitting last sc; join with sl st in first sc. Fasten off.

Finishing

Weave in all ends.

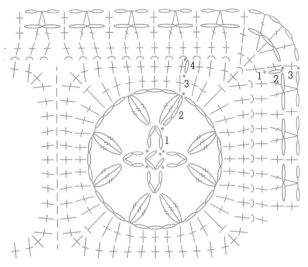

Edging Stitch Diagram

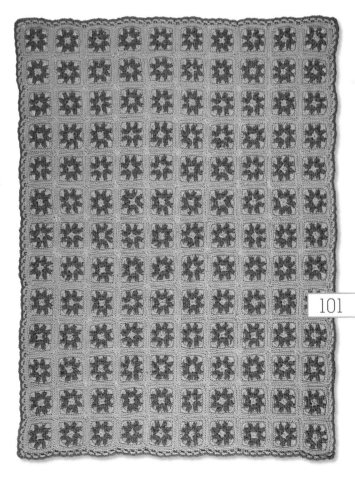

French Country

Skill level: Intermediate | Finished measurement: 41" × 57" (104cm × 145cm)

Imagine for a moment, an elegant table and chairs set in an open kitchen in the French countryside. The curtains billow with the breeze; succulent berries tumble out of a bowl next to a bright bunch of flowers.

Blue and yellow together makes me imagine how a home in the south of France might look.

GETTING STARTED

YARN

• Worsted weight yarn in 2 different colors (A and B)

The project shown was made using Caron Simply Soft (100% acrylic, 7oz/198g balls/364yd/ 333m) with 4 skeins in color 9945 sunshine (A) and 4 skeins in color 9710 country blue (B).

HOOK

• Size H/8 (5mm) crochet hook or any size to obtain gauge

• Size I/9 (5.5mm) crochet hook or any size to obtain gauge

• Size K/10½ (6.5mm) crochet hook or any size to obtain gauge

NOTIONS

• Yarn needle

GAUGE

• For this project, I recommend doing a swatch of each motif, changing hooks so the end result is that each square is the same size as the other two. All three squares must be the same size. This may take some finesse. Each complete square is 3½".

Notes: All rounds are worked on the right side. Make one of each motif first, noting the hook size used. Adjust hooks to get all three motifs the same size. Likely, Pick a Posie will require a smaller hook, like a H or I. Stain Berry and Chair Back will require a larger hook, like a J or K. Do not begin to produce motifs until you have worked out the sizing.

Motif A: Chair Back

Make 55.

With medium hook and color B, ch 3, join with sl st to form ring.

ROUND 1: Ch 1, (sc, ch 5) 4 times in ring; join with sl st in top of beg-sc—4 ch-5 sp and 4 sc. Fasten off.

ROUND 2: Join A with sc in any ch-5 sp, *ch 2, dc2tog placing first leg in same ch-5 sp and 2nd leg in next ch-5 sp, ch 2**, sc in ch-5 sp; rep from * 2 times, rep from * to ** once; join with sl st in top of beg-sc, do not fasten off—4 sc, 4 dc2tog, 8 ch-2 sp.

ROUND 3: Ch 1, 3 sc in first st, *3 sc in next ch-2 sp, sc in next st, 3 sc in next ch-2 sp**, 3 sc in next st; rep from * 2 more times, rep from * to ** once; join with sl st in first sc—40 sc. Fasten off.

ROUND 4: Join B with sc where previously fastened off, *3 sc in next st, sc in next 9 sts; rep from * 2 more times, 3 sc in next st, sc in last 8 sts; join with sl st in beg-sc—48 sc. Fasten off.

Motif B: Stain Berry

Make 55.

With largest hook and color A, ch 4, join with sl st to form ring.

ROUND 1: Beg-cl in ring, ch 3, (cl, ch 3) 3 times in ring; join with sl st in top of beg-cl—4 cl and 4 ch-3 sps. Fasten off.

ROUND 2: Join color B with sl st in any ch-3 sp; *ch 3, sl st in same sp, (sl st, ch 3, sl st) in next cl**, sl st in next ch-3 sp; rep from * 2 more times; rep from * to ** once; join with sl st in first sl st—8 ch-3 sps. Fasten off.

ROUND 3: Join A with sc in ch-3 sp over any cl; *ch 2, (2 dc, tr, 2 dc) in next ch-3 sp, ch 2**, sc in next ch-3 sp; rep from * 2 more times, rep from * to ** once, join with sl st in first sc, do not fasten off—4 sc, 8 dc, 4 tr, 8 ch-2 sps.

ROUND 4: Ch 1, sc in same st; *2 sc in ch-2 sp, sc in next 2 sts, 3 sc in next st, sc in next 2 sts, 2 sc in ch-2 sp**, sc in next st; rep from * 2 more times; rep from * to ** once; join with sl st in first sc—48 sc. Fasten off.

Motif C: Pick a Posie

Make 55.

With smallest hook and color A, ch 4 join with sl st to form ring.

ROUND 1: Ch 1, 8 sc in ring; join with sl st in beg-sc—8 sc. Fasten off.

ROUND 2: Join B with sc in any st, sc in same st; 2 sc in each of next 7 sts; join with sl st in first sc—16 sc. Fasten off.

ROUND 3: Join A with sc in any st, ch 3; (sc, ch 3) in each of next 15 sts; join with sl st in first sc—16 sc, 16 ch-3 sps. Fasten off.

ROUND 4: Join B with sc in any sc, ch 4; *sc in next sc, ch 4, rep from * 14 times; join with sl st in first sc—16 sc, 16 ch-4 sp. Fasten off.

ROUND 5: Working behind sts in round 4, join A with sc in any ch-3 sp of round 3; *ch 6, sk all sts on round 4, sk 3 ch-3 sps on round 3**, sc in next ch-3 sp of round 3, rep from * 2 times; rep from * to ** once; join with sl st in first sc, do not fasten off—4 sc, 4 ch-6 sps.

ROUND 6: Ch 3 (counts as dc), 2 dc in same st; *7 dc in next ch-6 sp, 3 dc in next st; rep from * 2 times, 7 dc in next ch-6 sp; join with sl st in top of beg ch-3—40 dc. Fasten off.

ROUND 7: Join B with sc in middle dc of 3-dc corner, 2 sc in same st; *sc in next 9 sts, 3 sc in next st; rep from * 2 times, sc in last 9 sts; join with sl st in beg-sc—48 sc. Fasten off.

Assembly

With yarn needle and B, with right sides facing each other, through both loops and both thicknesses, whipstitch motifs together according to the assembly diagram below.

A	B	C	A	B	C	A	B	C	A	B
C	A	B	C	A	B	C	A	B	C	A
B	C	A	B	C	A	B	C	A	B	C
A	B	C	A	B	C	A	B	C	A	B
C	A	B	C	A	B	C	A	B	C	A
B	C	A	B	C	A	B	C	A	B	C
A	B	C	A	B	C	A	B	C	A	B
C	A	B	C	A	B	C	A	B	C	A
B	C	A	B	C	A	B	C	A	B	C
A	B	C	A	B	C	A	B	C	A	B
C	A	B	C	A	B	C	A	B	C	A
B	C	A	B	C	A	B	C	A	B	C
A	B	C	A	B	C	A	B	C	A	B
C	A	B	C	A	B	C	A	B	C	A
B	C	A	B	C	A	B	C	A	B	C

Assembly Diagram

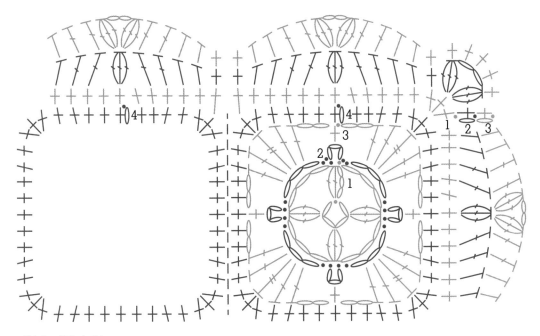

Edging Stitch Diagram

Edging

Note: All edging rounds are worked on the right side.

ROUND 1: With B, and largest hook, join with sc in middle sc of a corner starting a short side, 2 sc in same st; *sc in each st across, taking care to work 13 sc across side of each motif (including one sc from corner on end motifs)**, place 3 sc in middle sc of 3-sc corner; rep from * around, ending last rep at **; join with sl st in first sc, do not fasten off—680 sc.

ROUND 2: Ch 1, sc in first sc, **(cl, ch 2, cl) in next sc, *sc in next st, hdc in each of next 2 sts, dc in each of next 2 sts, sk 1 st, cl in next st, sk 1 st, dc in each of next 2 sts, hdc in each of next 2 sts, sc in next st; rep from * across to next corner; rep from ** around, omitting last sc; join with sl st in first sc. Do not fasten off.

ROUND 3: Ch 1, sc in first sc, **sc in next cl, 3 sc in next ch-2 sp, sc in next cl; *sc in next st, hdc in each of next 2 sts, dc in each of next 2 sts, (cl, ch 2, cl) in next cl, dc in each of next 2 sts, hdc in each of next 2 sts, sc in next st; rep from * across to next corner; rep from ** around, omitting last sc; join with sl st in first sc. Fasten off.

Finishing

Weave in all ends.

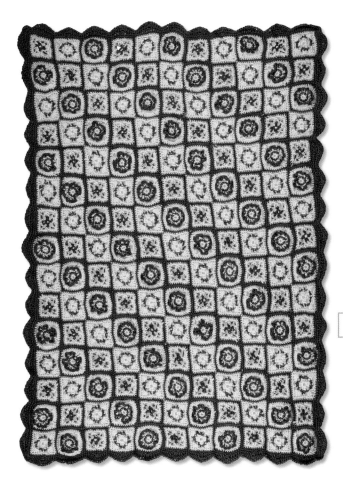

Brilliant Starburst

Skill level: Intermediate | Finished measurement: 49" × 67" (124cm × 170cm)

If I lie in my backyard and look up into the stars, I see the inspiration for this blanket. Like holding a prism up to the bright midnight stars, the starburst is brilliant and spellbinding. Which stars can you see from your part of the world?

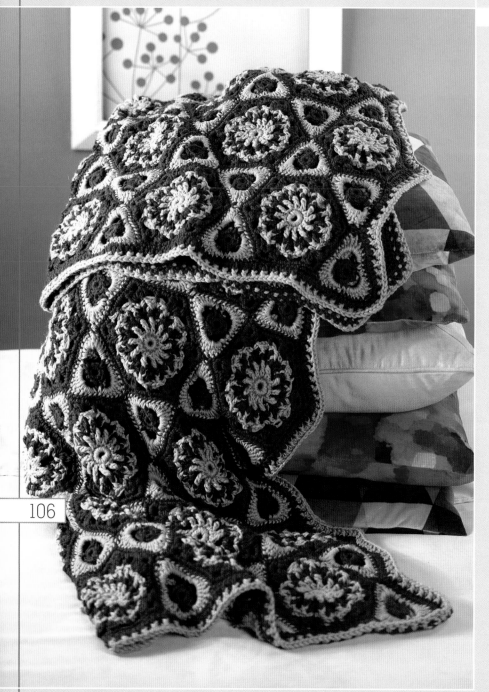

GETTING STARTED

YARN

• Worsted weight yarn in 2 different colors (A and B)

The project shown was made using Louet Gems Chunky (100% merino wool, 3.5oz/100g hanks/94yd/86m) with 12 hanks of color 66 bright blue (A) and 6 hanks of color 42 eggplant (B).

HOOK

• Size I/9 (5.5mm) crochet hook or any size to obtain gauge

• Size K/10½ (6.5mm) crochet hook or any size to obtain gauge

NOTIONS

• Yarn needle

GAUGE

• Hexagon with larger hook, rounds 1–2 in pattern = 3" (8cm)

Note: All rounds are worked on the right side.

Motif A: Brilliant Hexagon

Make 60.

With A, and larger hook, ch 5; join with sl st to form ring.

ROUND 1: Ch 1, 12 sc in ring; join with sl st in first sc, do not fasten off—12 sc.

ROUND 2: Ch 6 (counts as tr plus 2 ch); *tr in next st, ch 2; rep from * 10 more times; join with sl st in 4th ch of beg ch-6—12 tr, 12 ch-2 sps. Fasten off.

ROUND 3: Join B with sl st in any ch-2 sp, ch 5 (counts as dc plus 2 ch), dc in same sp; *FPdc around next tr, (dc, ch 2, dc) in next ch-2 sp; rep from * 10 more times; FPdc around next tr; join with sl st in 3rd ch of beg ch-5—12 FPdc, 24 dc. Fasten off.

ROUND 4: Join A with sc in any ch-2 sp, 2 more sc in same sp; *sk 1 st, FPdc around next st, sk 1 st, (sc, ch 2, sc) in next ch-2 sp, sk 1 st, FPdc around next st**, sk 1 st, 3 sc in next ch-2 sp; rep from * 4 more times; rep from * to ** once; join with sl st in first sc—60 sc, 12 FPdc and 6 ch-2 sps. Fasten off.

ROUND 5: Join B with sl st in the middle sc of any 3-sc group, ch 4 (counts as a hdc plus ch 2); *sk next 3 sts, (cl, ch 3, cl) in ch-2 sp, ch 2, sk 3 sts**, hdc in next sc, ch 2; rep from * 4 more times; rep from * to ** once; join with sl st in 2nd ch of beg ch-4, do not fasten off—12 cl, 6 hdc.

ROUND 6: Ch 1, sc in same st; *2 sc in ch-2 sp, sc in cl, 5 sc in ch-3 sp, sc in next st, 2 sc in ch-2 sp**, sc in next st; rep from * 4 more times; rep from * to ** once; join with sl st in first sc—72 sc. Fasten off.

Motif B: Serene Triangle

Make 120.

With A and smaller hook, ch 5; join with sl st to form ring.

ROUND 1: Ch 1, 9 sc in ring; join with sl st in first sc, do not fasten off—9 sc.

ROUND 2: Ch 1, sc in same st; ch 7, sk next 2 sts; *sc in next st, ch 7, sk 2 sts; rep from * 1 more time; join with sl st in first sc—3 sc, 3 ch-7 sps. Fasten off.

ROUND 3: Join B with sc in any ch-7 sp, (sc, 2 hdc, dc, tr, dc, 2 hdc, 2 sc) in same sp, sc in next st; *(2 sc, 2 hdc, dc, tr, dc, 2 hdc, 2 sc) in next ch-7 sp, sc in next st; rep from * 1 more time; join with sl st in first sc—3 tr, 6 dc, 12 hdc, 15 sc. Fasten off.

Finishing

Weave in all ends.

Assembly

To asemble the hexagons and triangles into a blanket, I suggest finding ways to make rows, then assembling the rows.

For our project, attach 2 triangles onto adjacent sides of each hexagon to form fish shapes: With yarn needle and A, holding right sides of one triangle and one hexagon together, matching stitches, whipstitch through both thicknesses. Repeat for second triangle onto same hexagon, placing the triangle on an adjacent side. It looks like a fish, doesn't it!

Line up all the fish into rows.

With yarn needle and A, holding right sides of each set together, matching stitches, whipstitch the fish together to form rows.

When all the sets are compiled into rows, line up the rows next to each other so that a triangle will be meeting a side of a hexagon. With right sides together, matching stitches, whipstitch the rows together.

Edging

Note: All edging rounds are worked on the right side.

ROUND 1: With A and smaller hook, join with sc in tr of a triangle's corner starting a long side, 2 more sc in same sp, sc in each st. At the join between two triangles, sc3tog, insert the hook into the tr st of the first triangle and pull up a loop, insert the hook into the middle sc on the hexagon and pull up a loop, insert the hook into the tr of the next triangle and pull up a loop, yo and pull through all loops on hook, continue placing 1 sc in each st except for the sc3tog that occur whenever two triangles join with a hexagon and the corners of a hexagon. At the corner of a hexagon, placing 3 sc in middle sc of sc-5 corner; at corners of remaining triangle, work 3 sc in corner sc. Continue in pattern around to first st; sl st in first sc. Do not fasten off.

ROUND 2: Ch 3 (counts as first dc), dc in each st around, placing 3 dc at each corner of hexagon and triangles; join with sl st in top of beg ch-3. Fasten off.

ROUND 3: With B and smaller hook, join B with sl st in st where previously fastened off, ch 2 (counts as hdc), hdc in next st, *in next st (and all corners) work: (FPdc, hdc, FPdc) around the same middle st of the dc-3 corner; (FPdc around next st, hdc in next st) across to next corner; rep from * around; join with sl st in top beg ch-2. Fasten off.

Finishing

Weave in all ends.

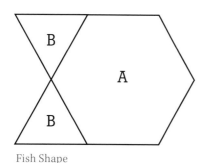

Fish Shape

Assembly Diagram

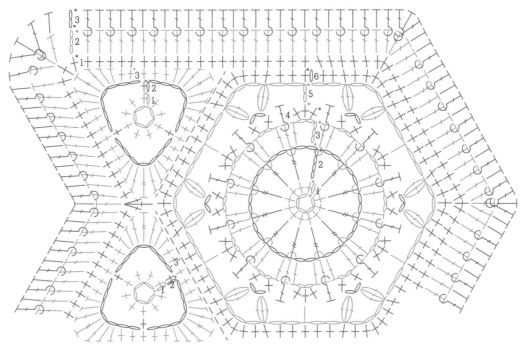

Edging Stitch Diagram

Ocean's Tide

Skill level: Intermediate | Finished measurement: 49" × 60" (124cm × 152cm)

The blue and green remind me of water and algae; the red reminds me of the red tide phenomena; and the flowing edging shows the ebb and flow of the dynamic nature of the ever-changing ocean.

GETTING STARTED

YARN
• Worsted weight yarn in 3 different colors (A, B and C)

The project shown was made using Bernat Satin (100% acrylic, 3.5oz/100g balls/163yd/149m) with 6 skeins of color 04531 rouge (A), 4 skeins of color 04222 fern (B) and 3 skeins of color 04141 sapphire (C).

HOOK
• Size K/10½ (6.5mm) crochet hook or any size to obtain gauge

NOTIONS
• Yarn needle

• Stitch markers (optional)

GAUGE
• Complete hexagon = 6" (15cm) (2 have 5 rounds, 1 has 6 rounds)

- beg pop = beginning popcorn
- pop = popcorn (5 dc)
- BPdc = Back Post double crochet
- sc2tog = single crochet decrease
- Rev sc = Reverse single crochet
- sc3tog = single crochet 3 together: [Insert hook in next st, yo, draw yarn through st] 3 times, yo, draw yarn through 4 loops on hook.

Note: All rounds are worked on the right side

Motif A: UFO Patch

Make 28

With A, ch 4, join with sl st to form ring.

ROUND 1: Ch 3 (counts as dc) 4 dc in ring; *ch 2, 5 dc in ring; rep from * once, ch 2; join with sl st in top of beg ch-3—15 dc, 3 ch-2 sps. Fasten off.

ROUND 2: Join B with sl st in 5th dc of a 5-dc group before any ch-2 corner sp, ch 3 (counts as dc) 4 dc in same st, ch 3, sk ch-2 sp, 5 dc in next st, ch 1, sk 3 sts, 5 dc in next st, ch 3, sk ch-2 sp, 5 dc in next st, ch 1, sk 3 sts, 5 dc in next st, ch 3, sk ch-2 sp, 5 dc in next st, ch 1; join with sl st in top of beg ch-3—30 dc, 3 ch-3 sps, 3 ch-1 sps. Fasten off.

ROUND 3: Working behind round 2, join A with sl st in any ch-2 sp in round 1, ch 4 (counts as tr), 4 tr in same sp, ch 3, sk 5 sts on round 2, 5 tr in middle dc of next 5-dc group in round 1, ch 3; *5 tr in next ch-2 sp on round 1, ch 3, 5 tr in middle dc of dc-5 group on round 1; rep from * 1 more time, ch 3; join with sl st in top of beg ch-4—30 tr, 6 ch-3 sps. Fasten off.

ROUND 4: Join C with sl st in same st as fasten off, ch 3, (counts as dc) dc in next 4 sts; *(2 dc, tr, 2 dc) in ch-3 corner sp, dc in next 5 sts; rep from * 4 more times; (2 dc, tr, 2 dc) in ch-3 sp; join with sl st in top beg ch-3—6 tr, 54 dc. Fasten off.

ROUND 5: Join B with sc in a corner tr prior to any ch-3 corner sp in round 2, 2 sc in same st; *sc in next 4 sts, working in front of round 3, long dc in next unused ch-3 sp in round 2, sk 1 st on round 4 behind dc just worked, sc in next 4 sts, 3 sc in next st, sc in each of next 9 sts**, 3 sc in next st; rep from * once; rep from * to ** once; join with sl st in first sc—3 dc, 69 sc. Fasten off.

Motif B: Twinkle

Make 28

With A, ch 4, join with sl st to form ring.

ROUND 1: Ch 3 (counts as first dc), 11 dc in ring; join with sl st in top beg ch-3, do not fasten off—12 dc.

ROUND 2: Ch 1, sc in first st, ch 7, sk 1 st; *sc in next st, ch 7, sk 1 st; rep from * 4 more times; join with sl st in first sc—6 sc, 6 ch-7 sps. Fasten off.

ROUND 3: Join B with sc in any sc, sc in next 7 ch sts; *sc in next sc, sc in next 7 ch sts; rep from * 4 more times; join with sl st in first sc—48 sc. Fasten off.

ROUND 4: Join A with sc in 4th sc of 7-sc side; *ch 3, sk 3 sc, dc in next st, ch 3**, sk 3 sts, sc in next sc; rep from * 4 more times, rep from * to ** once; join with sl st in first sc, do not fasten off—6 dc, 6 sc, 12 ch-3 sps.

ROUND 5: Ch 3 (counts as first dc), 2 dc in same st, 3 dc in next ch-3 sp, dc in next st, 3 dc in ch-3 sp; *3 dc in next st, 3 dc in ch-3 sp, dc in next st, 3 dc in ch-3 sp, 3 dc in next st; rep from * 4 more times; join with sl st in top of beg ch-3—60 dc. Fasten off.

ROUND 6: Join B with sc in middle dc of any 3-dc corner, 2 sc in same st, sc in next 9 sts; *3 sc in next sc, sc in next 9 sts; rep from * 4 more times; join with sl st in first sc—72 sc. Fasten off.

Motif C: Red Tide

Make 27

With A, ch 3, join with sl st to form ring.

ROUND 1: Ch 4 (counts as dc plus 1 ch), (dc, ch 1) 5 times in ring; join with sl st in 3rd ch of beg ch-4, do not fasten off—6 dc, 6 ch-1 sps.

ROUND 2: Beg pop in first st, ch 4, sk ch-1 sp; *pop in next st, ch 4, sk ch-1 sp; rep from * 4 more times; join with sl st in top of beg pop. Fasten off.

ROUND 3: Join B with sl st in any ch-4 sp, ch 4 (counts as first tr), 6 more tr in same sp; *ch 2, sk pop, 7 tr in next ch-4 sp; rep from * 4 more times, ch 2, sk pop; join with sl st in top of beg ch-4—42 tr, 6 ch-2 sps. Fasten off.

ROUND 4: Join C with sl st in any ch-2 sp, ch 3 (counts as dc), 2 dc in same sp, BPdc around next 7 sts, *3 dc in ch-2 sp, BPdc around next 7 sts, rep from * 4 times; join with sl st in top of beg ch-3—42 BPdc, 18 dc. Fasten off.

ROUND 5: Join A with sc in middle dc of any 3-dc- corner group, 2 sc in same st, sc in each of next 9 sts; *3 sc in next st, sc in each of next 9 sts; rep from * 4 more times; join with sl st in first sc—72 sc. Fasten off.

Assembly

Note: The UFO patch motifs are oriented randomly, with no particular orientation.

With motifs stacked in rows of 7 or 8 and yarn needle, with RS facing each other and A, through both loops of corresponding sts, whipstitch motifs together with short, easy horizontal joins until all strips are made.

When all the strips are made, lay out all the strips so that the short strips are between longer ones. Pin them together with locking stitch markers if it is easier to see where the points merge into the joins. Sew rows together.

Edging

Note: All edging rounds are worked on the right side.

ROUND 1: Join A with sc in any st, sc in each st around, working 3 sc in middle sc of each 3-sc corner, sc2tog in each junction between motifs, join with sl st in first sc. Fasten off.

ROUND 2: Join B with sc in any st, sc in each st around, working 3 sc in middle sc of each 3-sc corner, sc3tog in each junction between motifs, join with sl st in first sc. Fasten off.

ROUND 3: Join A with sl st in any st, ch 3 (counts as dc), *dc in each st to next corner, pop in middle st of 3-sc corner; rep from * around, dc in each st remaining st to beg; join with sl st in top of beg ch-3.

ROUND 4: Ch 1, sc in each st around, join with sl st in first sc.

ROUND 5: Ch 1, working from left to right, rev sc in each st around, join with sl st in first rev sc. Fasten off.

Finishing

Weave in all ends.

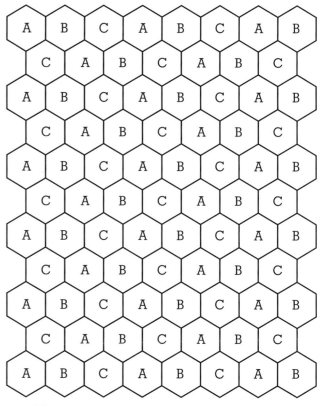

Assembly Diagram

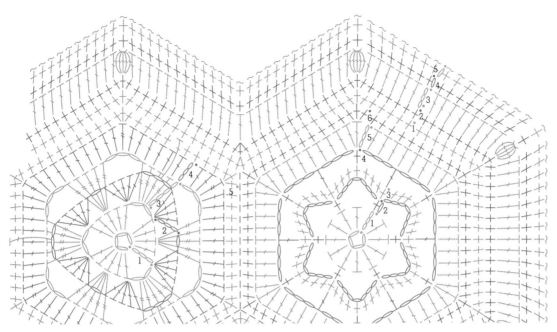

Edging Stitch Diagram

Spring Octagons

Skill level: Advanced | Finished measurement: 52" × 66" (132cm × 168cm)

This blanket is the ultimate in stash-busting projects! Use your scraps and unify the project with a neutral main color for stunning results. This project offers enough variety to keep you interested and enough repetition to keep progress flowing. Best yet, it's guaranteed to solicit "oohs" and "aahhs" from all who see it!

GETTING STARTED

YARN

- Worsted weight yarn in 4 different colors (A, B, C and D)

The project shown was made using Plymouth Encore (75% acrylic, 25% wool, 3.5oz/100g balls/200yd/183m) with 6 skeins in color 9408 light pink (A), 4 skeins in color 0215 yellow (B), 2 skeins in color 1317 teal (C) and 6 skeins in color 180 dark pink (D).

HOOK

- Size G/6 (4mm) crochet hook or any size to obtain correct gauge
- Size K/10½ (6.5mm) crochet hook or any size to obtain correct gauge
- Size J/10 (6mm) crochet hook or any size to obtain correct gauge

NOTIONS

- Yarn needle

GAUGE

- Each finished octagon should measure 6½" (17cm) from side to opposite side. More important than the number of inches is that all three motifs chosen need to be the same size so they will fit well together. The side of one square must equal the size of one side of the octagon in inches. The size must be finessed with gauge and hook.

114

Note: All rounds are worked on the right side in motifs A, B, C.

Motif A: Purple Pansy

Make 26.

With A, and middle-sized hook, ch 5; join with sl st to form ring.

ROUND 1: Beg-cl in ring, (ch 2, cl) 7 times in ring, ch 2; join with sl st in top of beg-cl—8 cl, 8 ch-2 sps. Fasten off.

ROUND 2: Join B with sl st in any ch-2 sp, ch 3 (counts as dc), 2 dc in same st; *ch 2, sk 1 cl, 3 dc in ch-2 sp; rep from * 6 more times, ch 2; join with sl st in top of beg ch-3—24 dc, 8 ch-2 sps. Fasten off.

ROUND 3: Join C with sc in any ch-2 sp, (ch 2, sc) in same sp; *sc in each of next 3 sts, (sc, ch 2, sc) in ch-2 sp; rep from * 6 more times; join with sl st in first sc—8 ch-2 sps, 40 sc. Fasten off.

ROUND 4: Join D with sl st in any ch-2 sp, ch 3 (counts as dc), 2 dc in same sp; *ch 2, FPdc in middle dc of 3-dc group in round 2, ch 2**, 3 dc in next ch-2 sp; rep from * 6 more times; rep from * to ** once; join with sl st in top beg ch-3, do not fasten off—24 dc, 8 FPdc, 16 ch-2 sps.

ROUND 5: Ch 1, sc in same st; *3 sc in next st, sc in next st, 3 hdc in ch-2 sp, hdc in next st, 3 hdc in ch-2 sp**, sc in next st; rep from * 6 more times; rep from * to ** 1 time; join with sl st in first sc—56 hdc, 40 sc. Fasten off.

Motif B: Purple Sunset

Make 27.

With B, and largest hook, ch 4, join with sl st to form ring.

ROUND 1: Ch 1, 8 sc in ring; join with sl st in first sc, do not fasten off—8 sc.

ROUND 2: Ch 4 (counts as tr), tr in same st; *ch 2, 2 tr in next st; rep from * 6 more times, ch 2; join with sl st in top of beg ch-4—16 tr, 8 ch-2 sps. Fasten off.

ROUND 3: Join C with sl st in any ch-2 sp, ch 3 (counts as dc) dc in next 2 sts; *(dc, ch 3, dc) in ch-2 sp, dc in each of next 2 sts; rep from * 6 more times, dc in ch-2 sp, ch 3; join with sl st in top of beg ch-3—32 dc, 8 ch-3 sps. Fasten off.

ROUND 4: Join D with sc in any ch-3 corner sp, 4 more sc in same sp; *ch 1, sk 1 st, sc in each of next 2 sts, ch 1, sk 1 st**, 5 sc in ch-3 sp; rep from * 6 more times; rep from * to ** 1 time; join with sl st in first sc, do not fasten off—56 sc, 16 ch-1 sps.

ROUND 5: Ch 1, sc in same st, sc in next st; *3 sc in next st, sc in each of next 2 sts, sc in ch-1 sp, ch 3, sk 2 sts, sc in ch-1 sp**, sc in each of next 2 sts; rep from * 6 more times; rep from * to ** once; join with sl st in first sc—8 ch-3 sps, 72 sc. Fasten off.

Motif C: Granny Octagon

Make 27.

With C and middle-sized hook, ch 4, join with sl st to form ring.

ROUND 1: Ch 3 (counts as dc), 2 dc in ring, ch 3; *3 dc in ring, ch 3; rep from * 2 more times; join with sl st in top of beg ch-3—12 dc, 4 ch-3 sp. Fasten off.

ROUND 2: Join B with sl st in any ch-3 sp, ch 3 (counts as dc), (2 dc, ch 3, 3 dc) in same sp; *ch 3, (3 dc, ch 3, 3 dc) in next ch-3 sp; rep from * 2 more times, ch 3; join with sl st in top of beg ch-3—24 dc, 8 ch-3 sps. Fasten off.

ROUND 3: Join A with sl st in any ch-3 sp, ch 3 (counts as dc), (2 dc, ch 3, 3 dc) in same sp; *ch 1, (3 dc, ch 3, 3 dc) in next ch-3 sp; rep from * 6 more times, ch 1; join with sl st in top of beg ch-3—48 dc, 8 ch-3 sps, 8 ch-1 sps. Fasten off.

ROUND 4: Join D with sl st in any ch-3 sp, ch 3 (counts as dc); *dc in each of next 7 sts, (dc, ch 3, dc) in ch-3 sp; rep from * 6 more times, dc in each of next 7 sts, (dc, ch 3) in ch-3 sp; join with sl st in top beg ch-3—8 ch-3 sps, 72 dc. Fasten off.

Motif D: Star Power

Make 63.

With B, and smallest hook, ch 4, join with sl st to form ring.

ROUND 1: (RS) Ch 1, 8 sc in ring; join with sl st in flp of first sc, do not fasten off—8 sc.

ROUND 2: (RS) *Ch 6, sl st in 2nd ch from hook (point of star ray), sc in next ch, hdc in next ch, dc in each of next 2 chs, sl st in flp of next sc in round 1; rep from * 7 more times—16 dc, 8 hdc, 8 sc, 8 sl st. Fasten off.

ROUND 3: With WS facing, join A with sc in any unused blp of round 2, sc in next unused blp; *ch 3, sc in each of next 2 unused blps; rep from * 2 more times, ch 3; join with sl st in first sc, do not fasten off—8 sc, 4 ch-3 sps.

ROUND 4: Ch 3 (counts as dc), turn; (2 dc, ch 3, 2 dc) in ch-3 sp; *dc in each of next 2 sts (2 dc, ch 3, 2 dc) in ch-3 sp; rep from * 2 more times, dc in last st; join with sl st in top of beg ch-3, do not fasten off—24 dc, 4 ch-3 sps.

ROUND 5: Ch 3, do not turn, dc in each of next 2 sts, 2 dc in ch-3 sp, sc in point of star ray, 2 dc in same ch-3 sp; *dc in each of next 3 sts, sc in point of next star ray, dc in each of next 3 sts, 2 dc in ch-3 sp, sc in point of next star ray, 2 dc in same ch-3 sp; rep from * 2 more times; join with sl st in top of beg ch-3—40 dc, 8 sc. Fasten off or proceed to inserting the square into the spaces left behind when the octagons are joined.

Assembly

Arrange octagons in 8 columns of 10 octagons each according to diagram.

With the wrong side of the blanket facing, A, and smallest hook, matching stitches, sc through the stitches of adjoining octagons and one side of a square with an exposed side of an octagon; join with sl st in first sc—48 sc. Fasten off. Repeat for all squares.

Edging

ROUND 1: With RS facing and middle-sized hook, join in any st with a sc, sc in each st around, place 3 sc in the middle sc of sc-3 corners, place 3 sc in ch-3 corner sps; join with sl st in first sc. Fasten off.

Finishing

Weave in all ends.

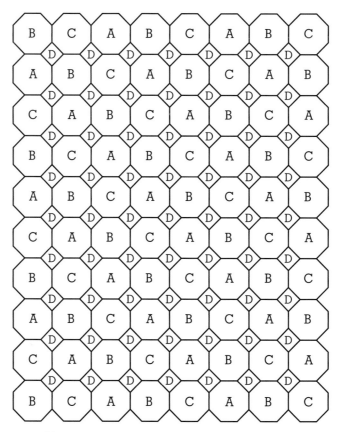

Assembly Diagram

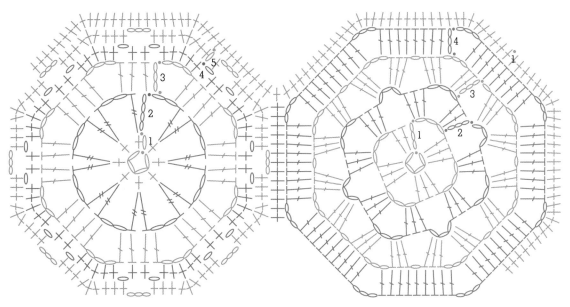

Edging Stitch Diagram

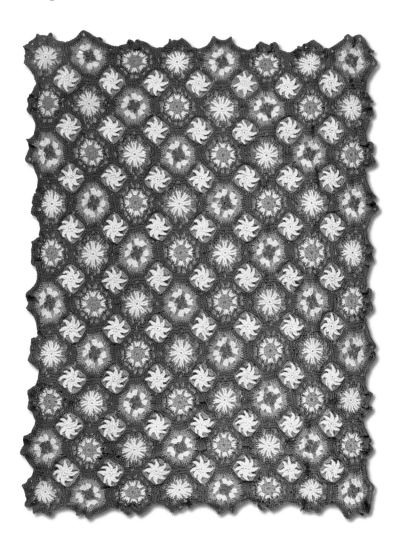

Yours Truly

Skill level: Advanced | Finished measurement: 55" × 60" (127cm × 152cm)

I laid these out in multiple configurations before choosing the basic checkerboard. The motifs seemed to vibrate before my eyes. I added an additional magenta round around every motif to give a flat space of color for the eyes to rest on and reduce the vibration.

When laid out, it looks like X's and O's. The motifs are joined on the top surface of the blanket—I love to do the join as a design element. It helps define the shape of the motif while allowing them to all work together as a whole.

GETTING STARTED

YARN

• Worsted weight yarn in 2 different colors (A and B)

The project shown was made using Lion Vanna's Choice (100% acrylic, 3.5oz/100g balls/170yd/ 156m) with 12 skeins of color 144 magenta (A) and 6 skeins of color 99 linen (B).

HOOK

• Size K/10½ (6.5mm) crochet hook or any size to obtain gauge

• Size J/10 (6 mm) crochet hook or any size to obtain gauge

NOTIONS

• Yarn needle

GAUGE

• Each complete motif is 5" × 5½" (11cm × 14cm)

• Motif A—Round 1 in pattern = 2½"

- FPdc = Front Post double crochet
- FPhdc = Front Post half double crochet
- FPdc2tog = Front Post double crochet decrease: [Yo, insert hook from front to back to front again around the post of next st, yo, draw yarn through st, yo, draw yarn through 2 loops on hook] twice, yo, draw yarn through 3 loops on hook.
- FPtr2tog = Front post treble crochet decrease: [Yo twice, insert hook from front to back to front again around the post of next st, yo, draw yarn through st, (yo, draw yarn through 2 loops on hook) twice] twice, yo, draw yarn through 3 loops on hook.

Note: All rounds are worked on the right side.

Motif A: Polka Dot

Make 55.

With A, ch 4, join with sl st to form ring.

ROUND 1: Ch 4 (counts as tr), 15 tr in ring; join with sl st in top beg ch-4—16 tr. Fasten off.

ROUND 2: Join B with sc in any st, ch 4, sk 3 sts, sc in next st, ch 3, sc in next st, ch 3, sk 1 st, sc in next st, ch 3, sc in next st, ch 4, sk 3 sts, sc in next st, ch 3, sc in next st, ch 3, sk 1 st, sc in next st, ch 3; join with sl st in first st, do not fasten off—8 sc, 2 ch-4 sps, 6 ch-3 sps.

ROUND 3: Ch 3 (counts as dc); *5 dc in ch-4 sp, dc in next st, ch 5, sk ch-3 sp, dc in next st, 3 dc in ch-3 sp, dc in next st, ch 5**, sk ch-3 sp, dc in next st; rep from * to ** once; join with sl st in top beg ch-3—24 dc, 4 ch-5 corner sps. Fasten off.

ROUND 4: Join A with sc in ch-5 corner sp before the fasten off, 6 sc in same sp; *sc in each of next 7 sts, 7 sc in ch-5 sp, sc in each of next 5 sts**, 7 sc in ch-5 sp; rep from * to ** once; join with sl st in first sc, do not fasten off—52 sc.

ROUND 5: Ch 3, dc in next 2 sts, *(dc, hdc, sc) in next st, sc in each of next 13 sts, (dc, hdc, sc) in next st**, dc in each of next 11 sts, rep from * to ** once, sc in each of last 8 sts; join with sl st in first sc—4 hdc, 30 sc, 26 dc.

Motif B: Gift Package

Make 55.

With A, ch 4, join with sl st to form ring.

ROUND 1: Ch 1, 8 sc in ring; join with sl st in top first sc, do not fasten off—8 sc.

ROUND 2: Ch 1, sc in same st; *ch 3, sk 1 st, sc in next st, rep from * 2 more times, ch 3, sk 1 st, join with sl st in first sc—4 sc, 4 ch-3 sps. Fasten off.

ROUND 3: Join B with sl st in any ch-3 sp, ch 3 (counts as dc), 2 dc in same sp, ch 4, 5 dc in next ch-3 sp, ch 4, 3 dc in next ch-3 sp, ch 4, 5 dc in ch-3 sp, ch 4; join with sl st in top of beg ch-3—16 dc, 4 ch-4 sps. Fasten off.

ROUND 4: Join A with sl st in a ch-4 sp starting a short side, ch 3 (counts as dc), 4 dc in same sp, ch 3, sk 3 sts, 5 dc in next ch-4 sp, ch 4, sk 5 sts, 5 dc in next ch-4 sp, ch 3, sk 3 sts, 5 dc in next ch-4 sp, ch 4, sk 5 sts; join with sl st in top of beg ch-3—20 dc, 2 ch-3 sps, 2 ch-4 sps. Fasten off.

ROUND 5: Join B with sl st in middle dc of either 5-dc corner starting a short side, ch 3 (counts as dc) 2 dc in same st, dc in each of next 2 sts, dc in ch-3 sp, FPtr2tog around the first and third dc directly below on round 3, dc in same ch-3 sp, dc in next 2 sts, 3 dc in next st, dc in next 2 sts, FPtr in dc directly below on round 3, 3 dc in ch-3 sp, FPtr in dc directly below on round 3, dc in next 2 sts, 3 dc in next st, dc in each of next 2 sts, dc in ch-3 sp, FPtr2tog around the first and third dc directly below on round 3, dc in same ch-3 sp, dc in next 2 sts, 3 dc in next st, dc in next 2 st, FPtr in dc directly below on round 3, 3 dc in ch-3 sp, FPtr in dc directly below on round 3, dc in last 2 sts; join with sl st in top of beg ch-3—2 FPtr2tog, 4 FPtr, 38 dc. Fasten off.

ROUND 6: Join A with sc in middle dc of a 3-dc corner starting a short side, 2 sc in same st, sc in each of next 4 sts, FPhdc around next st, sc in each of next 4 sts, 3 sc in next st, sc in each of next 3 sts, FPhdc in next st, sc in each of next 3 sts, FPhdc in next st, sc in each of next 3 sts, 3 sc in next st, sc in each of next 4 sts, FPhdc in next st, sc in next 4 sts, 3 sc in next st, sc in each of next 3 sts, FPhdc around next st, sc in next 3 sts, FPhdc around next st, sc in each of last 3 sts; join with sl st in first sc, do not fasten off—6 FPhdc, 46 sc.

ROUND 7: Ch 1, sc in same st, *(sc, hdc, dc) in next st, dc in each of next 11 sts, (dc, hdc, sc) in next st, sc in each of next 13 sts; rep from * once, omitting last sc join with sl st in first sc—4 hdc, 30 sc, 26 dc. Fasten off.

Finishing

Weave in all ends.

Assembly

With A and larger hook, arrange motifs into 10 columns of 11 rectangles, with the rectangles oriented in a portrait (vertical) manner, with WS facing each other, sc through inner loops only, matching stitches.

Edging

ROUND 1: With A, join with sc in middle st of either corner beginning a short side, 2 more sc in same st, *work 18 sc across each motif to next corner, 3 sc in middle st of next corner, work 15 sc across each motif to next corner*, 3 sc in middle st of next corner; rep from * to * once; join with sl st in first sc—694 sc. Fasten off.

ROUND 2: Join B with sc and any st, sc in each sc around, working 3 sc in each corner st, join with sl st in first sc.

ROUND 3: Join A with sl st in middle sc of any 3-sc corner, ch 4 (counts as first tr), 8 more tr in same st; *sk 3 sts, sc in each st across to last 3 sts before next corner, sk next 3 sts**, 9 tr in middle sc of next 3-sc corner; rep from * around, ending last rep at **, sl st in top of beg ch-4. Fasten off.

Finishing

Weave in all ends.

A	B	A	B	A	B	A	B	A	B
B	A	B	A	B	A	B	A	B	A
A	B	A	B	A	B	A	B	A	B
B	A	B	A	B	A	B	A	B	A
A	B	A	B	A	B	A	B	A	B
B	A	B	A	B	A	B	A	B	A
A	B	A	B	A	B	A	B	A	B
B	A	B	A	B	A	B	A	B	A
A	B	A	B	A	B	A	B	A	B
B	A	B	A	B	A	B	A	B	A
A	B	A	B	A	B	A	B	A	B

Assembly Diagram

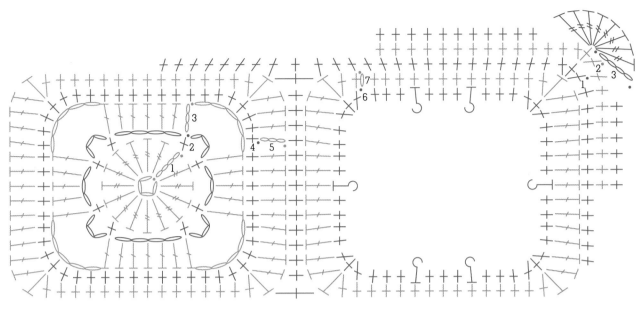

Edging Stitch Diagram

All Call

Skill level: Very advanced | Finished measurement: 38" × 40" (97cm × 102cm)

WARNING: Are you ready for a crochet throw-down? This project incorporates at least one of every motif in the book. The assembly of this project is very advanced and will require a degree of crochet intuition. The general assembly techniques will be described,

but there isn't enough room in this book to describe each join on each side of each motif. Swatching and blocking will be required to achieve consistent sizing among the fifty motifs. Do you have it in you? Go for it!

GETTING STARTED

YARN

• Worsted weight yarn in 1 color

The project shown was made using Lorna's Laces Shepherd Worsted (100% superwash wool, 4oz/114g hanks/225yd/206m) with 8 hanks in color #0 natural.

HOOK

• Swatching will be required to get all 50 motifs to match up in physical size. The stitches will all match up, but your gauge may vary from motif to motif.

• Sizes G, H, I, J, K crochet hooks or any size to obtain correct gauge

NOTIONS

• Yarn needle

GAUGE

• Target: Each motif, regardless of shape, should have each side that is as close to 2.5" (6cm) as possible. Switch hooks if necessary to achieve this target side length.

Notes: All rounds, including edging, are worked on the right side, except for the Star Power Motif. Leave long 8" (20cm) tails on all motifs. If necessary, the final round of a motif can be partially unraveled so that it can be used for sewing or joining.

Motifs

On page 124 is a chart of how many of each motif to make, which hook was used in the model for each motif and the motif's numerical location in the Assembly Diagram (page 125). Numbers on the left correspond to numbers on the Assembly Diagram.

Make and block all motifs before assembly.

Assembly

Assemble the motifs following the Assembly Diagram. On the Assembly Diagram, each location is given a number. In location 1 is Polka Dot, in location 2 is Harvest, etc.

Refer to the Assembly Tips for suggestions on how to join your motifs.

Edging

ROUND 1: Using I hook, join with sc in any corner, 2 more sc in same st; *sc in each st to next corner, place 3 sc in middle st of each corner and point; rep from * for remaining sides; join with sl st in first st, do not fasten off.

ROUND 2: Ch 3, (counts as first dc), dc in each st around all sides, do not add sts in the corners and points; join with sl st in top beg ch-3, do not fasten off.

ROUND 3: Ch 1, sc in same st, (ch 2, sc) in same st, sk 1 st; *(sc, ch 2, sc) in next st, sk 1 st; rep from * all around; join with sl st in first st. Fasten off.

Finishing

Weave in all ends.

ASSEMBLY TIPS

• Lay out the motifs working from the center outward following the Assembly Diagram. Start with the octagons and squares first.

• When motifs have a straight edge, they are easily joined by whipstitching or crocheting together.

• When a motif with an irregular edge is matched with a motif with an irregular edge, join them as you go.

• When a motif with an irregular edge is matched with a motif with a straight edge, join at the middle stitch of the corners.

• Where multiple motifs come together at one point, attempt to whipstitch or crochet through all the middle stitches of all the motifs to insure a tight join that does not leave a hole.

• If the motifs are stitched together too tightly, puckering will result.

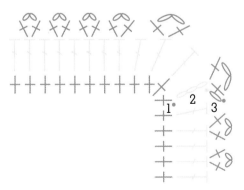

Edging Stitch Diagram

Number	Motif	Hook	Make
1, 26, 65	Polka Dot	I	3
2, 83	Harvest	J	2
3, 63	Beveled	J	2
4, 89	Twinkle	J	2
5, 82	Campfire	J	2
6	Flowery Day	K	1
7	Off Center	J	1
8, 81	Brilliant	J	2
9	Try-It Triangle	I	1
10, 87	Golden Hexagon	J	2
11, 49, 57	Oval in a Rectangle	I	3
12, 64	Neapolitan	I	1
13, 18	Acapulco	I	2
14, 60	Chair Back	H	2
15, 59	Flower Patch	I	2
16, 47	Eyelets	H	2
17, 61	Pick a Posie	H	2
19, 50	South Beach	I	2
20, 79	Vintage	K	2
21, 25	Red Tide	I	2
22	Purple Pansy	I	1
23, 69	Rose Octagon	J	2
24	Purple Sunset	I	1
27, 34	Gift Package	I	2
28, 48	Recycle	J	2
29, 74	Cherry Cordial	J	2
30, 45, 75	Stain Berry	J	3

Number	Motif	Hook	Make
31, 76	Puddles Gather Rain	J	2
32, 62	Oscar Square	I	2
33, 84	Whimsy	J	2
35, 56	Thumbprint	H	2
36, 55	Hurricane	J	2
37	Drama Queen	J	1
38	Oro Sol	I	1
39, 68	Floral Octagon	1	2
40, 85	Wrought Iron	J	2
41, 42	Last Blueberry	J	2
43, 86, 88	Simplicity	J	3
44, 77	Star Power	H	2
46	Team Captain	H	1
51, 70	Bluebonnet	J	2
52	Octagon Medallion	I	1
53	Raspberry Tart	J	1
54	Granny Octagon	I	1
58, 78	Floating Triangle	I	2
66	UFO Patch	J	1
67	Red Light, Green Light	I	1
71, 80	Scary Fun	H	2
72, 90	Cameo	H	2
73	Serene	J	1

Assembly Diagram

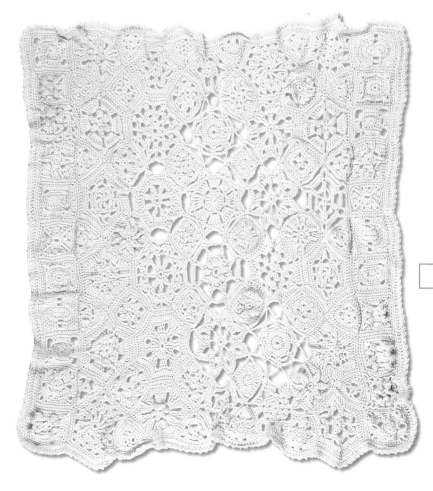

YARN WEIGHT GUIDELINES

Since the names given to different weights of yarn can vary widely depending on the country of origin or the yarn manufacturer's preference, the Craft Yarn Council of America has put together a standard yarn weight system to impose a bit of order on the sometimes unruly yarn labels. Look for a picture of a skein of yarn with a number 0–6 on most kinds of yarn to figure out its "official" weight. The information in the chart below is taken from www.yarnstandards.com.

	Super Bulky (6)	Bulky (5)	Medium (4)	Light (3)	Fine (2)	Superfine (1)	Lace (0)
Weight	super-chunky, bulky, roving	chunky, craft, rug	worsted, afghan, aran	light worsted, DK	sport, baby, 4ply	sock, fingering, 2ply, 3ply	fingering, 10-count crochet thread
Crochet Gauge Range*	5–9 sts	8–11 sts	11–14 sts	12–17 sts	16–20 sts	21–32 sts	32–42 sts
Recommended Hook Range**	M–13 and larger (9mm and larger)	K–10½ to M–13 (6.5mm–9mm)	I–9 to K–10½ (5.5mm–6.5mm)	7 to I–9 (4.5mm–5.5mm)	E–4 to 7 (3.5mm–4.5mm)	B–1 to E–4 (2.25mm–3.5mm)	Steel*** 6, 7, 8 Regular hook B–1 (1.4mm–2.25mm)

Notes:

* Gauge (what UK crocheters call "tension") is measured over 4in/10cm in single crochet (except for Lace [0], which is worked in double crochet)

** US hook sizes are given first, with UK equivalents in parentheses

*** Steel crochet hooks are sized differently from regular hooks—the higher the number, the smaller the hook, which is the reverse of regular hook sizing

US Crochet term		UK Crochet term
slip stitch (sl st)	• or —	slip stitch (ss)
single crochet (sc)	+	double crochet (dc)
half-double crochet (hdc)	T	half treble (htr)
double crochet (dc)	T	treble (tr)
treble crochet (tr)	T	double treble (dtr)

CROCHET HOOK CONVERSIONS

US SIZE	DIAMETER (MM)
B/1	2.25
C/2	2.75
D/3	3.25
E/4	3.5
F/5	3.75
G/6	4
H/8	5
I/9	5.5
J/10	6
K/10½	6.5
L/11	8
M/13, N/13	9
N/15, P/15	10
P/Q	15
Q	16
S	19

SUBSTITUTING YARNS

If you substitute yarn, be sure to select a yarn of the same weight as the yarn recommended for the project. Even after checking that the recommended gauge on the yarn you plan to substitute is the same as for the yarn listed in the pattern, make sure to crochet a swatch to ensure that the yarn and hook you are using will produce the correct gauge.

Resources

Bernat
Box 40, 320 Livingstone Ave South
Listowel, ON N4W 3H3
800-368-8401
www.bernat.com

Blue Sky Alpacas
PO Box 88
Cedar, MN 55011
888-460-8862
www.blueskyalpacas.com
(for Blue Sky Alpacas and Spud & Chloe)

Caron International
PO Box 222
Washington, NC 27889
800-862-5348
www.caron.com

Coats & Clark
PO Box 12229
Greenville, SC 29612
800-648-1479
www.coatsandclark.com
(for Red Heart, TLC and Stitch Nation)

Lion Brand Yarn
135 Kero Road
Carlstadt, NJ 07072
800-258-9276
www.lionbrand.com

Lorna's Laces Yarns
4229 North Honore Street
Chicago, IL 60613
773-935-3803
www.lornaslaces.net

Louet North America
3425 Hands Rd.
Prescott, ON K0E 1T0
800-897-6444
www.louet.com

Plymouth Yarn Company
500 Lafayette Street
Bristol, PA 19007
215-788-0459
www.plymouthyarn.com

Universal Yarn
284 Ann Street
Concord, NC 28025
877-864-9276
www.universalyarn.com

Index

More Crochet Titles to Keep You Going

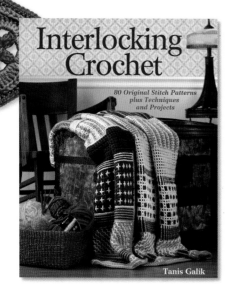

INTERLOCKING CROCHET

80 Original Stitch Patterns Plus Techniques and Projects

Tanis Galik

Learn to create incredible crochet projects that will leave even experienced crocheters amazed. Try the technique of interlocking crochet, which takes simple stitches and turns them into richly textured, reversible fabrics. There has never been a book that explores this technique so thoroughly. Try your hand (and crochet hook!) at this unique and interesting technique—you might never want to go back to regular crochet again!

paperback; 8" × 10"; 128 pages
ISBN-10: 1-4402-1239-2
ISBN-13: 978-1-4402-1239-0
SRN: Z7442

CROCHET NOW!

29 Projects for Baby, Home, Gifts and More

Candi Jensen

This book compiles the crochet patterns featured in season 3 of *Knit and Crochet Now*, the top knit and crochet show on PBS. Patterns from popular designers for everything from scarves and a purse, to afghans, pillows and jewelry are included. A basic technique section gives you the information you need to get started or freshen up your skills. The book also includes a DVD featuring the television segments for 12 crochet afghan squares from season 3.

paperback+DVD; 8.25" × 10.875"; 128 pages
ISBN-10: 1-4402-1388-7
ISBN-13: 978-1-4402-1388-5
SRN: Z7967

VINTAGE CROCHET FOR YOUR HOME

Best Loved Patterns for Afghans, Rugs and More from 1920–1959

Coats & Clark

In *Vintage Crochet for Your Home*, you will learn to create 30 projects for your home—shopping bags, potholders, placemats, afghans and more—all from the Coats & Clark pattern archives. Photos and illustrations show projects as they were first created, but each pattern has been updated with modern-day instructions, yarn recommendations and fresh, beautiful colors!

paperback; 8" × 10"; 144 pages
ISBN-10: 1-4402-1370-4
ISBN-13: 978-1-4402-1370-0
SRN: Z8579

These and other fine Krause Publications titles are available at your local craft retailer, bookstore or online supplier, or visit our website at www.mycraftivitystore.com.